Unchained Expectations

James Perry

Unchained Expectations

Library of Congress Control Number: 2018909892

ISBN 9781732437920

This book is dedicated to my four children

Elizabeth Lee Perry Barron (Beth)

James Andrew Perry (Andy)

Martha Ruth Perry Davis (Martha)

Rebecca Lois Perry Buice Taggart (Becca)

In behalf of our children, the Scriptures always present in the mind of Peggy and I are those recorded in:
Psalm 127:3
"Children are a heritage from the LORD."
and
Psalm 128:3
"Your children are like olive plants all around your table."

The Prayer We/They Sometimes Sang
Can a little child like me, Thank the Father fittingly?
Yes, oh yes! be good and true, Faithful, kind, in all you do;
Love the Lord, and do your part;
Learn to say with all your heart,
Father, we thank Thee, Father, we thank Thee,
Father in Heaven, we thank Thee.

Foreword

Through the ages, there have been wise servants of the living God who have boldly proclaimed that Christian living is not difficult, but it is impossible! In spite of all the resources God has made available for the continual growth and advancement of His redeemed, in the faith revealed in Holy Scripture, no one can consistently move ahead except by the continual application of divine precepts that can seal God's directives in the areas where they need to be applied.

It is not sufficient for one to be sufficiently aware of all the perilous elements that make their appeals to the population of any human society, anywhere on earth. It's imperative that those desirous of living a life pleasing unto God, and fully satisfactory unto themselves, be on their guard at all times. Dangers combated in the past may have disappeared from view, but they remain fully available, repackaged for greater appeal to its many potential users.

People need not merely to know how to interpret Holy Scripture accurately, but also to exegete the world and see how truth is being eroded, while blatant evil is being accepted by many as if it were beneficial for its consumers. In the godless world which we all occupy, so much that the Bible introduces as being bad is being accepted as good, while a great deal of evil is more and more being promoted as if it were good, and worthy of wider acceptation!

While solid Christian pulpits continue to dispense God's unchanging Truth as revealed in the pages of Holy Scripture, other institutions of contemporary society subtly (and often not so subtly) continue aggressively to make their appeals via the manifold media outlets through which citizens are being influenced.

Many who nurture their souls through regular reading and study of Holy Scripture, occasionally stumble when they encounter alternative offers which blatantly contradict the clear message of the Bible, adding confusion to those who should be growing in its knowledge and application.

Thank God that someone like Rev. James Perry, the author of this precious volume, brings his knowledge of God's Holy Word, combined with his many years of faithful pastoral ministry, to instruct and encourage contemporary Christians in knowing what's happening in the world, as well as how to counteract the manifold, insidious appeals of the wicked one in his attempts to deceive many when their own faith falters.

The author not only bases his arguments in the infallible, inerrant Word of God which he faithfully interprets and applies, but also with his up-to-date understanding of new trends in society, contemporary philosophies, and fallible notions about reality which seek to influence contemporary thought and action, while negating God's unchanging Truth!

Although his voice is just one among many others, I strongly recommend his pastoral approach and wise counsel to all who wish to lead a life of personal fulfillment, which also pleases our Lord.

While it may be true that Christian living in today's world is not just difficult, but impossible, we also know that nothing is impossible for the Almighty, and He is the One Who dwells in His redeemed through the Holy Spirit Who has been sent, to guide us into all truth, and enable us to refrain from all evil and do what is good which always pleases Him.

I wish a life of steady growth to all readers as they ponder the wise counsel the author faithfully offers with clarity in the pages that follow. God desires that His people be each day farther ahead of where they had been the day before, until the moment when their faith turns to sight, the indignities of this current life in the world no longer affect us, and only bliss prevails as His redeemed enjoy what Jesus has prepared for all who have embraced His eternal salvation.

Rev. Dr. Synesio Lyra, Jr.
Coconut Creek, Florida

Dr. Synesio Lyra, Jr. has served the Lord in various ways throughout his life:

- He was born in Brazil but has resided in the USA for 60 years.
- For 23 years he had been a full-time theological professor and continued as a part-time faculty member of Reformed Theological Seminary when an extension existed in Boca Raton, FL.
- He has also served as professor at Columbia International University in Columbia, S.C. and, during his ministry at Coral Ridge Presbyterian Church, at Knox Theological Seminary.
- He received his education on four continents and spent one year as Visiting Professor in Singapore.
- He served as Minister of Education at the Crystal Cathedral in California, and Minister of Pastoral Care at Coral Ridge Presbyterian Church in Ft. Lauderdale, Florida.
- Twice each year he also ministers in Brazil through preaching, lecturing and consulting.
- He is the Author of: *Appetizers for the Soul: Positive Thoughts to Begin and End the Day.*

Table of Contents

Introduction

For a number of years, the United States has tolerated an exponential plague and blight within its borders. Both prescribed opioids and illegal drugs are being used excessively. The contemporary culture has allowed for and embraced various mood modifiers it believes will enhance life and allow for societal acceptance. With a porous Southwest border, not only are illegal (undocumented) aliens entering the country, members of drug cartels and human-trafficking groups are active within the country.

The drug cartel infiltration not only makes addictive drugs available, it also results in individuals becoming addicted, as well as altered behavior in the lives of many. NCADD (National Council on Alcoholism and Drug Dependence) has reported:

> *The use of alcohol and drugs can negatively affect all aspects of a person's life, impact their family, friends and community, and place an enormous burden on American society. One of the most significant areas of risk with the use of alcohol and drugs is the connection between alcohol, drugs and crime.*
>
> *Alcohol and drugs are implicated in an estimated 80% of offenses leading to incarceration in the United States such as domestic violence, driving while intoxicated, property offenses, drug offenses, and public-order offenses.*
>
> *Our nation's prison population has exploded beyond capacity and most inmates are in prison, in large part, because of substance abuse:*
>
> *80% of offenders abuse drugs or alcohol.*
>
> *Nearly 50% of jail and prison inmates are clinically addicted.*

Approximately 60% of individuals arrested for most types of crimes test positive for illegal drugs at arrest.

The reality is that people will become chained, shackled and enslaved by the increased availability of illicit drugs. These can become debilitating and prevent people, young and old, from the fulfillment of dreams and expectations. While these things are considered from a secular perspective, there is a spiritual factor as well. The Apostle Paul wrote, Ephesians 6:12 (NKJV),

For we do not wrestle against flesh and blood, but against principalities, against powers, against the rulers of the darkness of this age, against spiritual hosts of wickedness in the heavenly places.

There is an ongoing spiritual conflict orchestrated by the one who was called a liar and murderer (John 8:44); a roaring lion seeking someone to devour (First Peter 5:8); a schemer (Ephesians 6:11); and crafty (Second Corinthians 11:3).

For several years, Russ Taff has sung, *Praise The Lord*, a song that expresses the reality of the spiritual enemy and that which he endeavors to accomplish. Within the song are lyrics that are the expression of what the enemy hopes to achieve.

When you're up against a struggle,
that shatters all your dreams.

Mood modifiers will leave one in a wretched state of both mind and body. It will leave one with conflicted thoughts and hopelessness.

And your hopes have been cruelly crushed
by Satan's manifested schemes...

One can become disillusioned and susceptible to negativity. It will contribute to an altering of one's perspective and goal for life. It can become a major distraction in one's life.

And you feel the urge within you
to submit to earthly fear...

The negativity and altered perspective will lead one to fret; become anxious; and loss of being able to see light at the end of the tunnel. If at all possible, it would be vital for one to recall some spiritual instruction and guideline. Some references are: Psalm 37:1 (NIV), "Do not fret because of those who are evil." Psalm 37:7, "Do not fret when people succeed in their ways, when they carry out their wicked schemes." Psalm 37:8-9, "Do not fret—it leads only to evil. For those who are evil will be destroyed." Philippians 4:6, "Do not be anxious about anything."

Don't let the faith you're standing in
seem to disappear - Praise the Lord,
He will work through those who praise Him.

The lyric states a possibility for those who are pressured by the enemy on various fronts. The basic truth is to stand in your faith without fear or wavering. One's faith may be very small or weak. One can be filled with many doubts and fears. John Newton wrestled with these same issues of life. His hymn, Amazing Grace includes: "It was grace that taught my heart to fear and grace, my fears relieved...Through many dangers, toils and snares I have already come. It was grace that brought me safe thus far and grace will lead me home." The Russ Taff anthem also includes:

Now, Satan is a liar and he wants to make us think,
That we are paupers, when he knows himself
we're children of the King.

Part of the devil's ploy is to pressure one to think and believe opposites. It is the same tactic he used with Eve in the Garden of Eden when he raised a question intended to bring doubt and confusion into her mind in terms of what the right choice should be. The serpent asked: "Did God really say?" This was his subtle approach that gained entry into her thinking and the unwise choice being made. The antidote to this infiltration is expressed in the anthem:

So lift up the mighty shield of faith
for the battle must be won.

Amid all the conflicting propositions and confusion of one's mind, the Biblical principle stated in Second Chronicles 20:15 - must rise to the surface before a wrong choice is made, "This is what the Lord says to you: Do not be afraid or discouraged because of this vast army. For the battle is not yours, but God's." This truth is echoed in the anthem with words of fact, reality and hope:

We know that Jesus Christ has risen
and the work's already done.
Praise the Lord,
He will work through those who praise Him.

We need to understand and remember there is an enemy who walks about (stalking a prey) as a roaring lion seeking someone to devour (First Peter 5:8). He is known for his subtlety and craftiness and is relentless in his pursuit of the vulnerable. Second Corinthians 2:11 (NKJV) reminds us, "lest Satan should take advantage of us; for we are not ignorant of his devices (schemes)." A paraphrase (MSG) renders it, "We don't want to unwittingly give Satan an opening for yet more mischief—we're not oblivious to his sly ways!"

Years ago, Timothy Leary (1920-1996), a professor at Harvard University, influenced a generation of students to experiment with psychedelic drugs. The drug of choice was

LSD (Lysergic Acid Diethylamide). This drug is known for its psychological effects which could alter awareness of one's surroundings, perceptions and feelings as well as sensations and images that seemed to be real although they are not. Timothy Leary promoted it as a means of expanding one's intelligence and perceptions that would otherwise be unknown.

As then, modern times have addictive drugs that are used among a cross-section of the population. It has been suggested that when driving a vehicle, one in five of the vehicles one encounters on the roadway has a driver that is under the influence of something – ranging from alcohol to heroin/cocaine or meth amphetamines, etc.

Addictions are evident in other areas of life, such as pornography, pedophilia, child or spousal abuse, etc. In Galatians 5:16, Paul states a clear directive to all people, "Walk in the Spirit, and you shall not fulfill the lust of the flesh." He proceeds to indicate seventeen particular acts of the flesh, Galatians 5:19-21 (NKJV), anyone of which can become debilitating and addictive:

> *Now the works of the flesh are evident, which are: adultery, fornication, uncleanness, lewdness, idolatry, sorcery, hatred, contentions, jealousies, outbursts of wrath, selfish ambitions, dissensions, heresies, envy, murders, drunkenness, revelries, and the like; of which I tell you beforehand, just as I also told you in time past, that those who practice such things will not inherit the kingdom of God.*

The first group of the (four) works of the flesh (sins) listed are sexual in nature. Throughout the culture, there is a preoccupation with the titillating. Whether it is in the latest fashions, motion pictures, television programs, publications or pornography, the enemy of one's soul knows the precise areas of vulnerability in a person's life and will exploit it.

The second group of the works of the flesh (sins) are spiritual in nature. Galatians 5:20 groups them as, "Idolatry, witchcraft, hatred, variance, emulations, wrath, strife, seditions, heresies." This device of the enemy beguiles a person beyond the regular form of acceptable religious practice. It influences a person toward an expansion of enrichment, experimentation, possibility and experience.

The third group of the works of the flesh (sins) have a direct negative impact on those around and close to one. It has been said that these particular sins represent a level of selfishness on the part of those who partake of them or exercise them. Galatians 5:21 lists them: "envy, murders, drunkenness, revelries, and the like; of which I tell you beforehand, just as I also told you in time past, that those who practice such things will not inherit the kingdom of God."

The 17 mentioned sins are all capable of having one chained and in bondage. The result should be taken seriously and soberly, "those who practice such things will not inherit the kingdom of God." Additionally, Romans 1:18-32 lists those who have violated God's Word and Standards. As a result, God has turned away from them and given them up to pursue their alternative secular-carnal lifestyle. The NLT uses the phrase: "God abandoned them to do whatever shameful things their hearts desired." These are people who are chained, shackled and enslaved to and in their sinful choices. There is no limit to those things that chain and enslave one. Addictions come in a variety of practices and abuses - from drug addiction, alcoholism, spousal and child abuse, gambling, anger, pornography, sexual proclivities, self-centered lifestyle, etc. Some of these practices, habits, addictions and behaviors can include and result in imprisonment.

The latest available report of Prison Population (2018) includes:

> *The American criminal justice system holds more than 2.3 million people in 1,719 state prisons, 102 federal*

prisons, 901 juvenile correctional facilities, 3,163 local jails, and 76 Indian Country jails as well as in military prisons, immigration detention facilities, civil commitment centers, and prisons in the United States territories.

The report also states that the prison system is over-populated and under-staffed.

Two generations ago, chain gangs were a reality in certain parts of this nation. Prisoners were taken out of their cells and made to do menial tasks. Some of the tasks included roadside work. To make certain no one attempted to escape, the prisoners were shackled by a ball and chain. It served as a constant reminder of the dreadful choice that one had made to bring about being visibly chained.

In much the same way, the one who has succumbed to the works of the flesh, is similarly shackled by and to the enemy of one's soul. An illustration of this is the life of Calvin Hunt who came to know Christ as his Savior and Lord through the ministry of the Brooklyn Tabernacle in Brooklyn, NY. Calvin Hunt had a wife and children. He also lived in a nice apartment. However, he had an addiction – crack cocaine. He would leave the security and love of his home and go to a slum area where he would stand in line to get his fix of crack. More often than not, he would spend nights in a dog house behind the slum building where he had made his purchase. His wife and those at the Brooklyn Tabernacle prayed that God would deliver Calvin Hunt of his addiction and return him to his home and family. One Wednesday night, as they were praying, Calvin came walking down the aisle of the Church. He was embraced by the Pastor as he repented of his foolish choices and sins. His wife and children were over-joyed. All who were present rejoiced.

He had a strong singing voice and after his restoration to Jesus Christ and being restored with his family, his testimony was put to music and he would sing with great feeling and conviction these words:

There is a blood, a cleansing blood,
That flows from Calvary.
And in this blood, there's a saving power,
For it washes white and makes me clean.

Refrain:

I'm clean; I'm clean.
I've been washed in His blood.
I'm clean; I'm clean.
Through the power of His love.
I've been cleansed in the fountain
Of blood shed for me.
Oh, I'm clean.,
Through the blood of the Lamb.
I'm clean.

Only His blood, His cleansing blood,
Can wash my sins away.
For I stand today, with my heart so clean,
Through the blood that Jesus shed -
I'm truly, truly free!

I 'm clean, I'm clean,
Jesus blood has made me clean!
I'm clean!

Is there a way by which these chains that so easily bind one can be broken? Can one be unshackled and know what it means to be free indeed? Can one who has been defiled be cleansed? What is the way for this to happen? Jesus emphatically stated, John 8:31-36,

> *If you abide in My word, you are My disciples indeed. And you shall know the truth, and the truth shall make you free. They answered Him: We are*

Abraham's descendants, and have never been in bondage to anyone. How can You say, You will be made free? Jesus answered them: Most assuredly, I say to you, whoever commits sin is a slave of sin. And a slave does not abide in the house forever, but a son abides forever. Therefore if the Son makes you free, you shall be free indeed.

Charles Wesley's Hymn, And Can It Be? expresses this truth succinctly when he wrote,

And can it be that I should gain
An interest in the Savior's blood?

My chains fell off, my heart was free,
I rose, went forth, and followed Thee.

In a dramatic way, Peter experienced his chains falling off (Acts 12) as the people of God had gathered and prayed for his release from prison. In a similar way, the one who responds to the Gospel can find release from the dungeon of sin, be loosed, cleansed and set free from the chains that bind. Have you been set free by Jesus Christ? Have you been cleansed by Him and given new life?

The following Chapters will study some of the subtleties that enslave and the beauty of being unchained and set free by God's Grace. A stanza and refrain in the Hymn, At Calvary expresses:

Oh, the love that drew salvation's plan!
Oh, the grace that brought it down to man!
Oh, the mighty gulf that God did span
At Calvary!

Mercy there was great, and grace was free;
Pardon there was multiplied to me;

There my burdened soul found liberty
At Calvary.

1. Oppressiveness of Darkness

> *This is the message we have heard from him and proclaim to you, that God is light, and in him is no darkness at all. If we say we have fellowship with him while we walk in darkness, we lie and do not practice the truth. But if we walk in the light, as he is in the light, we have fellowship with one another, and the blood of Jesus his Son cleanses us from all sin.*
>
> First John 1:5-7 (ESV)

There are many references throughout the Bible regarding the prevailing darkness in the world. The references are to people, nations and cultures that have chosen a path that takes them away from the Lord and His Word. The clear definitive statement about light versus darkness is made by Jesus Christ (John 8:12) when He spoke to the people and said: "I am the light of the world. Whoever follows me will never walk in darkness but will have the light of life." This amplifies the introductory words in John 1:1-5 where the focus is on Jesus Christ,

> *In the beginning was the Word, and the Word was with God, and the Word was God. He was with God in the beginning. Through him all things were made; without him nothing was made that has been made. In him was life, and that life was the light of all mankind. The light shines in the darkness, and the darkness has not overcome it.*

John speaks of the light shining in darkness. He conveys the thought that the light is penetrating to the point where it can pierce through the darkness and the fog of mankind. It is sufficient to deliver one from the oppressiveness and captivity of darkness.

It is not unusual to for some people to have an innate dread or fear of darkness. There is the uncertainty of the unknown. Every sound or shadow increases the level of a person's anxiety. This apprehension is based upon the thought that something or someone is lurking in the darkness and will possibly cause personal harm. As frightened as some may be in the secular world, a glimpse into the spiritual is far more frightening and should cause many to come to The Light, Jesus Christ. Paul describes the spiritual struggle as (Ephesians 6:12), "our struggle is not against flesh and blood, but against the rulers, against the authorities, against the powers of this dark world and against the spiritual forces of evil in the heavenly realms." Elsewhere, he draws the contrast between the secular and spiritual when he wrote in Second Corinthians 6:14-7:1, "Do not be yoked together with unbelievers. For what do righteousness and wickedness have in common? Or what fellowship can light have with darkness? What harmony is there between Christ and Belial? Or what does a believer have in common with an unbeliever? What agreement is there between the temple of God and idols?"

Darkness conjures up all kinds of fear and trepidation in people. It is a fear of what is unseen and unknown. An example of this occurred while attending college. I worked part time on weekends as a night watchman in the women's dormitory. The responsibility entailed making rounds each hour at twelve designated check points. At a designated time, lights were to be out in all of the rooms throughout the building. As I made the rounds in the darkened building, every creak or sound that was heard was startling. Attention was supposed to be given to those sounds and the possible cause of them. One night, I accompanied an older staff member who had returned to the building at a later hour. I was struck by her obvious fear of walking down the dimly lighted hallway to her room. She requested that I escort her to her room and turn the lights on in her suite of rooms. After ascertaining that all was well, it struck me that there are people who have an abject fear of the darkness. The fear is not based upon what is known but the possibilities of what is unknown.

Martin Luther gave evidence of fearlessness and confidence when it came to the forces of darkness during the historic period known as The Protestant Reformation (1500 AD). When ordinary men might've trembled at the threats coming from the Church power structures, Martin Luther found his refuge in Psalm 46. Later, he wrote the hymn, A Mighty Fortress Is Our God. As he spelled out his spiritual journey in that Hymn, he confidently asserted his unchained expectation in the words of the third stanza,

And though this world, with devils filled,
Should threaten to undo us,
We will not fear, for God hath willed
His truth to triumph through us:
The Prince of Darkness grim, We tremble not for him;
His rage we can endure, For lo! his doom is sure,
One little word shall fell him.

He went on to indicate what that "one little word" was in the following stanza, "That word above all earthly powers, No thanks to them, abideth…" That word was based upon that which refocused him, Romans 1:17, "The just shall live by faith alone."

For Luther that meant the practical embrace of what would become known in theological studies as The Five Solas. They are five Latin phrases (or slogans) that emerged from the Protestant Reformation intended to summarize the Reformers' basic theological principles in contrast to certain teachings of the Roman Catholic Church of the day. "Sola" is

Latin meaning "alone" or "only" and the corresponding phrases are:

Sola Fide, by faith alone;
Sola Scriptura, by Scripture alone;
Solus Christus, through Christ alone;
Sola Gratia, by grace alone;
Soli Deo Gloria, glory to God alone.

These phrases may be found individually expressed in the various writings of the 16th century Reformers, either explicitly or implicitly" (Online: Theopedia, Creeds and Confessions). These truths undergird one who approaches God with unchained expectations.

In the Sermon on the Mount, Jesus makes reference to the distinction between light and darkness. The words of Jesus in Matthew 6:22-23 (ESV) are:

> *The eye is the lamp of the body. So, if your eye is healthy, your whole body will be full of light, but if your eye is bad, your whole body will be full of darkness. If then the light in you is darkness, how great is the darkness!*

The emphasis of Jesus Christ is precise. He expects His people represent Him by being full of light. This will be evidenced by one's conduct being disciplined, committed, regular and steady. To accomplish this result, one must adhere to Hebrews 12:2 and have one's eyes fixed on Jesus. He is the true light. No other light is needed nor should any alternative be sought. The eye of faith must be fixated on heaven and the one who is the True Light for the world (John 1:7-9.

In the 1980s, Frank Peretti wrote two novels that addressed Darkness (This Present Darkness and Piercing The Darkness).His point is that the spiritual warfare is real and the true light is the source for victory over the forces of evil and demons. The Library Journal (C. Robert Nixon) reviewed Peretti's writings and stated:

> *Peretti's writings are built upon fundamentalist Christian ideas. As it tells the story of Sally Roe, who goes from spiritualism to conversion, it also traces a battle to save a Christian school from demon-inspired litigation. The human activities are again overshadowed by the battle between angels and demons, whom the author takes quite literally, giving them names, personalities, and dialogue. They influence all human activities just as human prayer helps angels and hampers demons.*

Another commentator, an English art critic of the Victorian era, mused about darkness when he wrote:

> *Seeing falsely is worse than blindness. A man who is too dim-sighted to discern the road from the ditch, may feel which is which; but if the ditch appears manifestly to him to be the road, and the road to be the ditch, what shall become of him? False seeing is unseeing, on the negative side of blindness.*
>
> (John Ruskin, Modern Painters, 1843).

A comment attributed to Helen Keller states: "The only thing worse than being blind is having sight but no vision." Of all people, Helen Keller knew the value of light and benefits of light. When Jesus speaks of light, he has reference to the mind of one and principles that govern one's soul. If mind or soul is dark, how great is that darkness! We do well to think about light of the body, mind and soul in relationship to one's eye. Most know how calamitous it is when that light is irregular or extinguished, as when the eye is diseased or sight is lost. There is an increasing awareness about eye diseases in modern times. Physically, cataracts and molecular degeneration affect one's ability to see clearly. Treatment is available and can result in a degree of remedy.

Spiritually, if the light that should be present in one's mind and soul is diseased and neglected, darkness will be experience within. If the spiritual eye is not fixed on heaven how much darker and more dreadful will it be than any darkness of the eye! Paul wrote about the perpetrator of one's darkness, Second Corinthians 4:4, "The god of this age has blinded the minds of unbelievers so they cannot see the light of the gospel of the glory of Christ, who is the image of God."

Jesus speaks of one area that can bring spiritual darkness to the mind and soul of anyone. It is avarice (an extreme greed for wealth or material gain). It flows from and is a result of the prevailing darkness in the world and the covetous heart of mankind. Jesus addresses the misdirected of one's spiritual focus with material wealth and possessions (Matthew 6:24).

> *No one can serve two masters. Either you will hate the one and love the other, or you will be devoted to the one and despise the other. You cannot serve both God and money.*

Another illustration is given by Jesus when a rich young man comes to Him. The young man has endeavored to have a religious orientation and to do that which is correct. We read about him in Luke 18:18-27,

> *A certain ruler asked him, Good teacher, what must I do to inherit eternal life? Why do you call me good? Jesus answered. No one is good—except God alone. You know the commandments: You shall not commit adultery, you shall not murder, you shall not steal, you shall not give false testimony, honor your father and mother. All these I have kept since I was a boy, he said. When Jesus heard this, he said to him, you still lack one thing. Sell everything you have and give to the*

poor, and you will have treasure in heaven. Then come, follow me.

The decision that had to be made was between what a person is and has versus what a person should be and his personal view regarding what he could do with earthly possessions. Some wealthy people are alleged to have said regarding their personal gains and net worth, "If I can't take it with me, then I won't go." Ironically, at the funeral for wealthy people, there has never been a trailer filled with their assets and possessions they will take into eternity. The Apostle Paul wrote in a pastoral letter to Timothy where he offered the following comment about wealth. First Timothy 6:6-10 (NLT).

> *Yet true godliness with contentment is itself great wealth. After all, we brought nothing with us when we came into the world, and we can't take anything with us when we leave it. So if we have enough food and clothing, let us be content. But people who long to be rich fall into temptation and are trapped by many foolish and harmful desires that plunge them into ruin and destruction. For the love of money is the root of all kinds of evil. And some people, craving money, have wandered from the true faith and pierced themselves with many sorrows.*

These words to Timothy were the words that needed to be impacting the rich young ruler in Luke 18. His perspective had become focused on the secular rather than the spiritual. He had not come to a place where he possessed unfettered and unchained expectations. Luke's account continues with the concerns of one who thinks he is free but who in actuality is bound in the vain approach of secular achievement and earthly possessions. Verses 23 through 27 indicate:

When he (the ruler) heard this, he became very sad, because he was very wealthy. Jesus looked at him and said: How hard it is for the rich to enter the kingdom of God! Indeed, it is easier for a camel to go through the eye of a needle than for someone who is rich to enter the kingdom of God. Those who heard this asked: Who then can be saved? Jesus replied: What is impossible with man is possible with God.

Jesus indicates that a person of wealth has a difficult time when it comes to spiritual commitment. While it may be difficult, Jesus adds that it is not in the "impossible" category. There is hope for all who seek Him and find Him. The sin of avarice is akin to other sins. In the 4th Century, someone compiled a listing of the Seven Deadly Sins. In no special order they were: Pride, Greed, Lust, Malicious Envy, Gluttony, Wrath and Sloth. The listing of sins can never be complete. There are so many forms of temptation and variants when it comes to sin.

For those with physical blindness or afflicted by visual limitation, it is acknowledged to be a difficult plight. Alternatives for those with visual limitations include access to resources including large print Bibles and other books. For those who are totally blind, there is the possibility of audio books and other materials, as well as the possibility for learning to utilize braille publications. For those with spiritual blindness, it is also a difficult plight. There are no resources to which one can turn for assistance with spiritual blindness. Rather than a resource, it is through the only Source, Jesus Christ, where satisfaction and deliverance can be found. In the colleges I attended, the school Hymn (written by Mary D. James – 1871) was, "All for Jesus." The third stanza contains these defining words:

Worldlings prize their gems of beauty,
Cling to gilded toys of dust,

Boast of wealth and fame and pleasure;
Only Jesus will I trust.

A spiritual application is given by the prophet of God in a day of evil and oppression. It is the Lord's indictment upon a rebellious generation. They had numerous opportunities of turning to the Lord and walking in His ways. Despite the gracious acts of the Lord's compassion, the people had chosen to ignore Him. The Lord sends Isaiah to convey His message. The descriptive language used, Isaiah 59:1-10 (ESV), is an indictment against the people,

> *Behold, the Lord's hand is not shortened, that it cannot save, or his ear dull, that it cannot hear; but your iniquities have made a separation between you and your God, and your sins have hidden his face from you so that he does not hear. For your hands are defiled with blood and your fingers with iniquity; your lips have spoken lies; your tongue mutters wickedness. No one enters suit justly; no one goes to law honestly; they rely on empty pleas, they speak lies, they conceive mischief and give birth to iniquity...The way of peace they do not know, and there is no justice in their paths; they have made their roads crooked; no one who treads on them knows peace. Therefore, justice is far from us, and righteousness does not overtake us; we hope for light, and behold, darkness, and for brightness, but we walk in gloom. We grope for the wall like the blind; we grope like those who have no eyes; we stumble at noon as in the twilight, among those in full vigor we are like dead men.*

If we come boldly to The Lord with unchained expectancy, we will realize the certainty of being free indeed from unintended consequences. The issue is between secular and spiritual; wrong and right; man's way or God's way.

There is no need or benefit from living like those who are characterized by the words: We grope for the wall like the blind; we grope like those who have no eyes; we stumble at noon as in the twilight, among those in full vigor we are like dead men.

When I wrote the book, Navigating The Cultural Maze, the summary shared the reason and objective for that writing:

> *The world is facing considerable turmoil and challenge. Ebola, a disease in West Africa has affected eight nations, with the major impact areas in Guinea, Sierra Leone and Liberia. The United States has had to cope with a different type of disease - demonstrations, riots, looting and violence in several cities. A description of the cause and effect of these times is addressed in Isaiah 59:13-15 regarding the behavior of people who are sliding toward and into the cultural maze, "Transgressing and denying the Lord, and turning away from our God, speaking oppression and revolt, conceiving in and uttering from the heart lying words. Justice is turned back, and righteousness stands far away; for truth has stumbled in the streets, and uprightness cannot enter. Yes, truth is lacking; and he who turns aside from evil makes himself a prey. Now the Lord saw, and it was displeasing in His sight that there was no justice." The church has this moment to be the light it was intended to be. It must shine into and penetrate the darkness so that people will be led away from and out of the cultural maze. This book will provide you with challenging insights and encouragement to be a light shining into and piercing the darkness of your day.*

In the book's introduction, I summarized the only possible direction and path one can follow in life. It is either the pathway of light and guidance by God or darkness and rejection of anything to do with the true light. I wrote:

> *The plight of those who have chosen the path of darkness is summarized in Psalm 107:10-12 (NIV): "Some sat in darkness and the deepest gloom, prisoners suffering in iron chains, for they had rebelled against the words of God and despised the counsel of the Most High. So he subjected them to bitter labor; they stumbled (fell down), and there was no one to help." This was the temporal consequence for the choices made: (a) their rebellion against the Word of God and (b) they despised the counsel of the Most High God. The bondage was grueling and grievous. Their lives were marked by oppression and hardship.*

What was needed then for their lives is the same as what the culture of this day needs, being set free from the stranglehold of darkness and to realize the full dimension of unchained expectations in the true light. How can a person change direction and course in life? What is required to escape from the cultural maze of darkness and the related bondage in that state? I wrote in Navigating the Cultural Maze,

However, in the midst of their distress, they came to their senses and remembered the right thing to do. Psalm 107:13-14 (NIV),

> *Then they cried to the Lord in their trouble, and he saved them from their distress. He brought them out of darkness and the deepest gloom and broke away their chains.*

One must turn to the Lord in true faith. Once that occurs there is also a new reality: "He brought them out of darkness and the deepest gloom and broke away their chains." I find myself returning frequently for the reminder contained in the

Charles Wesley Hymn, "And Can It Be?" because it serves as a song of victory and commitment for the follower of Jesus Christ:

My chains fell off, my heart was free,
I rose, went forth, and followed Thee.

May these words written by Charles Wesley serve as a summary of your unchained expectancy and life of victory. Have you been set free by Jesus Christ? Have you been unchained and unshackled by Him? Are your eyes fixed upon the true light, Jesus Christ? Why is this necessary and important? Escaping the cultural maze of darkness as one comes to the true light, Jesus Christ, is the starting point on the path of living not somehow but triumphantly.

There is a Gospel song by Zach Williams that asserts one can find deliverance for one's needs in and by one person, Jesus Christ alone.

If you've been walking the same old road
for miles and miles;
If you've been hearing the same old voice
tell the same old lies...
There's a better life...
If you need freedom or saving -
Jesus Christ is a prison-shaking Savior.
If you've got chains -
Jesus Christ is a chain breaker.

2. Adverserial Ambitions

Peter, an apostle of Jesus Christ, To God's elect, exiles scattered throughout the provinces of Pontus, Galatia, Cappadocia, Asia and Bithynia, who have been chosen according to the foreknowledge of God the Father, through the sanctifying work of the Spirit, to be obedient to Jesus Christ and sprinkled with his blood: Grace and peace be yours in abundance.

First Peter 1:1-2 (NIV)

For the people of God in the First Century Church, the times were sobering and severe. It was a time of fear, threat and upheaval. Persecution was taking place by the dictate of the Emperor of Rome against Biblical Christians. Out of necessity, they were being scattered into other provinces that were not yet hostile to them. They left behind their homes and most of their possessions. The first reason for persecution came when fires broke out in Rome during the summer of A.D. 64 when Nero was Emperor (A.D. 54-67). He confiscated private property whenever he pleased, executing those who resisted. The fires resulted from Nero's dream of rebuilding Rome into a monument to his greatness. He envisioned great palaces, temples and marble buildings. The fires destroyed about 40% of the city. He believed that the fires and rebuilding the city would be met with approval and personal popularity. When that did not occur, he chose to blame the cause of the fires on the Christians in Rome. The government began to arrest and cruelly tortured believers. During this time of persecution, Nero's minions hunted down and executed Peter and Paul because they had been defined as sect leaders.

Later in the first century, another Emperor, Domitian (A.D. 81-96), instituted a more severe persecution. Domitian saw Christianity as an unlicensed religion and ordered its persecution in A.D. 91. This persecution arose partly because of Domitian's insistence that he be recognized as deity prior to his death. Additionally, he disdained Jews and hated anything Jewish. Since Christianity had Jewish roots, the persecutions included Christians as much as Jews. During Domitian's persecution of the Jews and Christians, the aged Apostle John was banished to the Isle of Patmos. In this time of exile, he had the visions that were written down and became the Book of Revelation in the Holy Scriptures. Many of his words in Revelation bear directly on the intensity of Domitian's persecution. He wrote (Revelation 17:5-6), "Babylon the great, the mother of prostitutes (harlots) and of the abominations of the earth. I saw that the woman was drunk with the blood of God's holy people, the blood of those (the martyrs) who bore testimony to Jesus."

Regardless of the difficult times being endured by Jewish converts, Peter wanted them to live, act and deal appropriately. He wanted them to be cognizant of the basic reality that there is an adversary who is relentless and ruthless in his desire to destroy the Church and all Christians. The words of hope and challenge were stated by him in First Peter 5:6-11 (ESV),

> *Humble yourselves, therefore, under the mighty hand of God so that at the proper time he may exalt you, casting all your anxieties on him, because he cares for you. Be sober-minded; be watchful. Your adversary the devil prowls around like a roaring lion, seeking someone to devour. Resist him, firm in your faith, knowing that the same kinds of suffering are being experienced by your brotherhood throughout the world. And after you have suffered a little while, the God of all grace, who has called you to his eternal*

glory in Christ, will himself restore, confirm, strengthen, and establish you. To him be the dominion forever and ever. Amen.

Are you prepared to face a similar challenge and resist the adversary of this day? Will you be committed to Jesus Christ and fight the good fight of faith for His name and glory? Your unchained expectation should be in Jesus Christ alone regardless of any cost or sacrifice. Great challenges should evoke greater commitment and resistance.

Many years ago while living in St. Louis, MO, we took our young children to the St. Louis zoo. A lioness had given birth to a litter of cubs and they were on display in the lion house. The cubs were in a playpen near the zookeeper's office. They were playful and looked cuddly. While the spectators were viewing the cubs, the lioness was stalking back and forth in her cage and roaring very loudly. Doubtlessly, it was all she could do to be protective of her cubs. The lion house seemed to tremble with her loud roaring. Our eldest daughter was about four years of age and amid the roaring of the lioness, she became frightened and ran toward me and leaped into my arms, hugging me tightly about my neck. In her father's arms, she felt protected and safe. The verses above, especially verses 8-9, have a forceful application for all of us in all generations:

Be sober-minded; be watchful.
Your adversary the devil prowls around like a roaring lion, seeking someone to devour. Resist him, firm in your faith.

How do we react to the adversary's stalking and roaring like a lion? Do we have any fear of his capability and design for the human race? At such a moment, do we run to our Heavenly Father and leap into His strong arms and hug Him tightly around His neck? Do we come to Him immediately for His strength, protection and safety?

The question needing an answer is: Are we prepared and ready to respond to the adversary's confrontations and challenges? If so, how, when and in what way? One practical beginning point is: What does the Bible mean to you right now? How well and how much do you honor it daily? In Jeremiah 15:16, we get a glimpse of the prophet's quiet moment when he is alone with the Lord. Jeremiah said:

> *Your words were found, and I ate them, and your words became to me a joy and the delight of my heart, for I am called by your name, O Lord, God of hosts.*

We are not required literally to eat the pages of our Bibles. We are, however, to consume the words of scripture as we ingest its meaning and application. It should result in our cherishing God's Word in our heart and life. When Jesus prayed for his followers, John 17:17, He prayed in terms of how they were to use God's Word and how it was to impact their life. That same prayer is applicable to all biblical Christians today: "Sanctify them in the truth; Your Word is truth."

A trend of the 21st Century is to remove the Bible from public view or prominence. The cultural influences have been wreaking havoc within the general public and, to a degree, within the local churches of our land. One of the recent efforts is removing and banning the Bible from Public and School Libraries. A news item on April 11, 2016 indicated:

> *One the latest list of books most objected to at public schools and libraries, one title has been targeted nationwide, at times for the sex and violence it contains, but mostly for the legal issues it raises is: The Bible.*

It finished sixth on a list of 10 books to be excluded. What is the rightful place for the Holy Scriptures? Should it be easily accessible in public libraries? Is it something that you cherish and faithfully read/study?

In a blog posted November 2007, titled Fractured Foundations, I wrote:

A long time ago, a friend shared with me words that he had written in the front of his Bible. He allowed me to copy it and write it in the front of my personal Bible. It asked a basic question: How should I approach the Bible? The answer given is:

Think of it carefully; Study it prayerfully!
Deep in your heart let its oracles dwell!
Ponder its mystery; Slight not its history.
For none ever loved it too fondly or well!

This is in keeping with the words of Psalm 119:11, "I have stored up Your Word in my heart, that I might not sin against You." Also, Psalm 119:105, "Your word is a lamp to my feet and a light to my path." The words of a hymn about the Bible should be learned and sung in a stirring and triumphant manner. It references the Bible as a rock and a firm foundation. It speaks of the Bible as the truth eternal that counters all error and falsehood. It was written by: Haldor Lillenas (1917):

The Bible stands like a rock undaunted
'Mid the raging storms of time;
Its pages burn with the truth eternal,
and they glow with a light sublime.

The bible stands though the hills may tumble,
It will firmly stand when the earth shall crumble;
I will plant my feet on its firm foundation,
for the Bible stands.

Another stanza adds,

The Bible stands every test we give it,
For its Author is divine;

By grace alone I expect to live it,
and to prove and to make it mine.

The adversary is very patient and equally persistent. In the past two generations, we have seen laws enacted ranging from abortion on demand to the current day transgender bathroom controversy. The adversary's scheming is similar to dripping water. It is to erode the Biblical core and moral values until they are moot or no more. Is the adversary succeeding? Yes! Is the church at large losing its effectiveness and impact? Yes! Are professing Christians becoming more lackadaisical about core values, foundational principles and moral standards? Yes!

It is important for every professing Christian to know that we have a very active adversary, and are aware of the objectives and tactics he employs. In different settings and situations, his tactics will vary. First of all, Genesis 3:1-4 reveals to us that he is sly and crafty. The text states:

> *Now the serpent was craftier than any of the wild animals the Lord God had made. he said to the woman, did God really say, you must not eat from any tree in the garden? The woman said to the serpent, we may eat fruit from the trees in the garden, but God did say, you must not eat fruit from the tree that is in the middle of the garden, and you must not touch it, or you will die. You will not certainly die, the serpent said to the woman. for God knows that when you eat from it your eyes will be opened, and you will be like God, knowing good and evil.*

The serpent's defining profile is in the description: "The serpent was craftier." He slithers around the professing Christian to seek and find a point of vulnerability. He then crafts his presentation in a believable and palatable manner. It is to the end that the professing Christian will question a value or standard of God and succumb to the adversary's point of view.

In addition to the adversary being crafty, he employs similar tactics when he tempts a person to other negative behaviors. When he appeared to Jesus Christ after He had fasted forty days and nights, Matthew 4:1-11, he tries to lure Jesus Christ into what he considers to be points of vulnerability. The three general areas of temptation both for Jesus Christ and the professing Christian are the same. The areas are summarized in First John 2:15-17,

> *Do not love the world or anything in the world. if anyone loves the world, the love of the father is not in him. for all that is in the world - the desires (lusts) of the flesh, the desires (lusts) of the eyes, and the (boastful) pride of life - is not from the father but from the world. The world is passing away along with its desires, but whoever does the will of God remains forever.*

A parallel passage is Psalm 1:1-2,

> *Blessed is the one who does not walk in step with the wicked or stand in the way that sinners take or sit in the company of mockers, but whose delight is in the law of the Lord, and who meditates on His law day and night.*

The aim of the Psalmist is to remind us of the progressive danger of any accommodation with those places and things that should be identified as danger zones. The directive of the Psalm regarding temptation and sin is threefold:

(1) Do not walk in or near the places that are dominated by wickedness, sin and unrighteousness;

(2) Do not stand and observe the ways of the wicked; and

(3) Do not permit yourself to sit with or among those who make a mockery of sin and God's standards.

Note the adversary's approach when he sets out to tempt Jesus, Matthew 4:1-11. He seeks to tempt Him in three primary areas. The first is where he believes Jesus would be most vulnerable, the lust of the flesh. His approach might've been along the lines of, "You've fasted 40 days and nights and You're hungry, famished."

If You are the Son of God, as You claim to be, you have the power and right to command the stones on the ground to become bread. Everyone will understand that You only did it because You were hungry. Jesus responds (Vs. 4, NLT), "No! The Scriptures say, People do not live by bread alone, but by every word that comes from the mouth of God" (Deuteronomy 8:3).

Undaunted, the adversary advances to the lust of the eyes. He takes Jesus to the city of Jerusalem. At the highest point of the Temple, the adversary tersely states to Jesus, "If you are the Son of God, jump off." In his craftiness and deceitfulness, the adversary quotes a portion of Scripture (NLT - Psalm 91:5-6): "He will order his angels to protect you. and they will hold you up with their hands so you won't even hurt your foot on a stone." Jesus quickly responded (Verse 7), "The Scriptures also say, 'You must not test the

The third area of temptation deals with the ego, the boastful pride of life. (Vs. 8) "Next the devil took him to the peak of a very high mountain and showed him all the kingdoms of the world and their glory." His clear objective from the beginning of these temptations are now disclosed. The adversary's final approach is (Verse 9), "I will give all these kingdoms to you." The price for yielding to this temptation: "If you will kneel down and worship me." If Jesus Christ yields to this final temptation, the entire purpose of redemption will be thwarted and the adversary will be victorious. Jesus does not hesitate in His response (Verse 10), "Get out of here, Satan, for the Scriptures state, you must worship the Lord your God and serve only him" (Deuteronomy 6:13).

When the adversary was unsuccessful with his schemes, deceptions and temptations, we note (Verse 11) "Then the devil went away, and angels came and took care of Jesus." A lesson we can learn from the temptation of Jesus Christ is that He always quickly referenced Scripture in His rebuttal to the adversary's advances. The other lesson we should glean from this is that the adversary is very real and persistent. A promise has been given for the Biblical Christian. When the adversary comes, we can rest assured in the promise about our Advocate with the Father, Jesus Christ the righteous one. Two passages to keep in mind are, First John 2:1-2 (NIV),

> *My dear children, I write this to you so that you will not sin. But if anybody does sin, we have an advocate with the Father—Jesus Christ, the Righteous One. He is the atoning sacrifice for our sins, and not only for ours but also for the sins of the whole world.*

Whenever the adversary attempts to convince you of his ways versus God's way, or with any other enticement to lead you away from the will and purpose of God for your life, your Advocate is close by and ready to deliver you. You should always remember the truth of our second passage,

> *Therefore, let anyone who thinks that he stands take heed lest he fall. No temptation has overtaken you that is not common to man. God is faithful, and he will not let you be tempted beyond your ability, but with the temptation he will also provide the way of escape, that you may be able to endure it.*

These words should solidify for you the truth in the model prayer Jesus taught His disciples. In Matthew 6:11 (ESV) are these words: "And lead us not into temptation, but deliver us from evil." The paraphrase of this prayer (NLT) is, "And don't let us yield to temptation, but rescue us from the evil one." The thrust is similar with either of these versions. The idea is that temptation is real and stronger than we can humanly prevent. We need The Advocate to keep us from yielding. We need Him to rescue us from the evil one.

Several years ago, Dr. A. W. Tozer wrote a book titled: I Talk Back to the Devil: The Fighting Fervor of the Victorious Christian (The Tozer Pulpit). The introduction for this writing included:

> *The highest that can be said of any creature is that it fulfilled the purpose for which God made it. What is holding you back from being all God wants you to be? Are you still holding on to past sins? Do memories of your spiritual failures haunt you? Or maybe you want to stay in control and not become one of those "fanatical" Christians? It is one of the devil's oldest tricks to discourage the saints by causing them to look back at what they were. Indeed, Satan has been in the business of intimidating and deceiving the people of God for a very long time. But as we press toward maturity in Christ, we are armed with great strength to engage in battle with that great Adversary. We can stand up to the Devil and shout "I am a child of God! I will not take this any longer, and I remind you that the forgiveness and cleansing I have freely received comes from Jesus Christ!*

You can talk back to the Devil, but will you? The victorious Christian life is possible and necessary. In my first pastorate, there was a dear and faithful woman of God. Despite personal issues that could've been discouragements or excuses, she began each day reading the Word of God and saying a simple prayer based upon Deuteronomy 33:25, O Lord, You have promised in Your Word, "as your days so shall your strength be." You have given me another day and I need Your strength for it. She wanted to live her life in close relationship with her Advocate with the Father, Jesus Christ her Savior and Lord. She wanted to live each day – not somehow, but triumphantly! As Dr. Tozer asked: "What is holding you back from being all God wants you to be?"

If you come to The Advocate, you can do so with unchained expectancy. He will keep you from enslavement to sin and bondage to the enemy of your soul. He will grant you the reality of being free indeed in Him.

How firm a foundation, ye saints of the Lord,
is laid for your faith in His excellent Word!
What more can He say than to you He hath said,
who unto the Savior for refuge have fled?

3. Adverserial Accusations

And I heard a loud voice in heaven, saying: Now have come the salvation and the power and the kingdom of our God, and the authority of His Christ. For the accuser of our brothers has been thrown down, he who accuses them day and night before our God. They have conquered him by the blood of the Lamb and by the word of their testimony; and they did not love their lives so as to shy away from death.

Revelation 12:10-11 (ESV)

The adversary is not only crafty, deceitful and subtle, but relentless in his desire and effort to cause personal rebellion against God, His values, His Word and His standards. He will accuse God's people and even come before God with his irreverence and accusations. A classic example is shared in Job 1:6-12 (ESV). The text indicates,

> *Now there was a day when the sons of God came to present themselves before the Lord, and Satan also came among them. The Lord said to Satan, from where have you come? Satan answered the Lord and said, from going to and fro on the earth, and from walking up and down on it. And the Lord said to Satan, Have you considered my servant Job, that there is none like him on the earth, a blameless and upright man, who fears God and turns away from evil?*

This interaction will now take a pivotal turn.

> *Then Satan answered the Lord and said, Does Job fear God for no reason? Have you not put a hedge around him and his house and all that he has, on every side? You have blessed the work of his hands, and his*

possessions have increased in the land. But stretch out your hand and touch all that he has, and he will curse you to your face.

The Lord was not surprised by the adversary's words or duped into yielding to his request. The Lord knows His servant Job well and the reality of his commitment to the Lord. Even though it will cause grief and hardship, the Lord knows His servant will endure and be faithful regardless of the personal cost or inconvenience. The adversary is given permission by the Lord, with a restriction and limitation, to test Job.

And the Lord said to Satan, Behold, all that he has is in your hand. Only against him do not stretch out your hand. So Satan went out from the presence of the Lord.

The point of this chapter is not an exposition of the Book of Job but to illustrate the relentlessness and persistence of the adversary to cause defeat and denial in the lives of God's people. "Does Job fear God for nothing?" Satan is suggesting that Job is in a religious relationship for what he can gain from it. The Lord knows differently. The Lord knows that Job will persevere through any trial or adversity. He will be faithful regardless of the personal cost.

There is an interesting moment while Jesus was celebrating the Passover with His disciples. It will be the last time on earth that He will celebrate the Passover with them. The betrayal is about to happen and the crucifixion will soon follow. Luke 22:31-34 (ESV) contains the interesting statement by Jesus and a prophetic utterance by Him:

Simon, Simon, behold, Satan demanded to have you, that he might sift you like wheat, but I have prayed for you that your faith may not fail. And when you have turned again, strengthen your brothers.

When Jesus stated to Peter, Satan demanded to have you, the pronoun "you" is singular and direct that Peter is the one attached to Satan's demand. It also emphasizes a difference from seeking permission in Job 1 to the demand in Luke 22. The response of Peter is predictable and typical:

Peter said to him, "Lord, I am ready to go with you both to prison and to death."

There can be no doubt about the loyalty Peter wanted to have and the courage he would hope to display in the hour of trial or greatest need. It is a similar hope that the Biblical Christian would express. For Peter, it was not going to happen at this time and place. Jesus went on with His prophetic word to Peter: Jesus said, "I tell you, Peter, the rooster will not crow this day, until you deny three times that you know me."

Peter's unchained expectation is that Jesus would not be mistreated, arrested or put to death. He was sincere in his expressed desire to stand with Jesus Christ regardless of the personal cost, accusations or opposition. He was ready to defend Jesus. Peter would learn that the forces of evil would soon be unleashed against Jesus Christ. Peter would also learn something about himself. Fear would overcome him. He would deny ever having known or been with Jesus Christ. He would flee from the crucifixion site and hide with the others in a locked room. We can only wonder what we would've done if we were there and the angry mob was ready to inflict pain upon a loved one or on us personally.

Later on in his life, Peter would review with the believers who were being scattered because of persecution that which happened a few years earlier when Jesus Christ was crucified. He wrote in First Peter 1:18-21 (NASB):

> *Knowing that you were not redeemed with perishable things like silver or gold from your futile way of life inherited from your forefathers, but with precious blood, as of a lamb unblemished and spotless, the blood of Christ. For He was foreknown before the*

foundation of the world but has appeared in these last times for the sake of you who through Him are believers in God, who raised Him from the dead and gave Him glory, so that your faith and hope are in God.

It is clear that Peter came to an understanding that God's Covenant of Redemption was an eternal plan that was determined before the foundation of the world was created and fashioned. The crucifixion was not an accident but according to the foreordained plan of God.

One of the subtleties of the adversary is to infiltrate the unsuspecting in the Church, both secular or spiritual, to become complacent and detached from what is occurring in the Church and world. It is a form of gullibility and naiveté. Once a nation turns its back on God, the Church begins to feel the impact. Low attendance and shifting demographics, plus reduction in financial contributions are all factors that enter into the decision processes of the Church.

Accommodation becomes part of the modus operandi of the organization. Things that God has condemned, the Church begins to find ways to condone them. People both within and without the Church have the capacity to be duped into doing evil and causing harm to others. When Paul wrote his Pastoral Epistles to both Timothy and Titus, this type of behavioral shift was on his mind. He wrote, II Timothy 3:1-5 (NIV),

But understand this: In the last days terrible times will come. For men will be lovers of themselves, lovers of money, boastful, arrogant, abusive, disobedient to their parents, ungrateful, unholy, unloving, unforgiving, slanderous, without self-control, brutal, without love of good, traitorous, reckless, conceited, lovers of pleasure rather than lovers of God, having a

> *form of godliness but denying its power. Turn away from such as these!*

A study written several years ago by Warren Wiersbe was titled: The Strategy of Satan. A broad outline of his writing can be seen in the content of some of the Chapters of his book. Chapter One, Satan's identity is that he is a deceiver. His aim is to condition a person's mind so it will readily believe lies. Additionally, he wants those he attacks to be or become ignorant of God's will and purpose for one's life. Just as was indicated earlier, we can learn from Jesus' temptation that our best defense is a good offense based upon the inspired Word of God.

Another avenue of the adversary's subtlety is found in his identity as the destroyer. His target is the health and well-being of a person or family member. Any malady brought on by the adversary is to the end that a person knows the reality of suffering. The goal is to get the person to question God and to become resistant or impatient with God's will. Once again, we should always remember and bask in the love, mercy and grace of God.

God's people need to be equipped, prepared and ready to fight the good fight of faith. There are two passages God's people need to know and heed to fend off the adversary's assaults. The first text is Ephesians 6:10-18 where Paul writes to the believers how they can stand strong and withstand the assaults by the enemy. He wrote,

> *Finally, be strong in the Lord and in his mighty power. Put on the full armor of God, so that you can take your stand against the devil's schemes...Put on the full armor of God, so that when the day of evil comes, you may be able to stand your ground, and after you have done everything, to stand.*

Paul is indicating the avenues and means by which the fury of the enemy will be unleashed upon the people of God. He identifies the enemy and cites the direction from which attacks will ensue. He has stated clearly why God's people need the whole armor of God for their defense against all evil and wickedness. The purpose is to embolden one to take a stand against the devil's schemes. To be prepared and ready for whatever may come to pass, Paul urges, "And pray in the Spirit on all occasions with all kinds of prayers and requests. With this in mind, be alert and always keep on praying for all the Lord's people."

Another compelling passage is Second Corinthians 2:9-11 when Paul writes,

> *Another reason I wrote you was to see if you would stand the test and be obedient in everything. Anyone you forgive, I also forgive. And what I have forgiven, if there was anything to forgive, I have forgiven in the sight of Christ for your sake, in order that Satan might not outwit us. For we are not unaware of his schemes.*

Take a moment to digest the closing statement: "In order that Satan might not outwit us. For we are not unaware of his schemes." Satan will outwit us if he can. His schemes are complex and appear to make sense. He will endeavor to convince one that it is alright to pursue alternatives to God's standards and values.

A third emphasis in the Wiersbe book focuses the rule the adversary seeks in your life. He wants to appeal to your will so that it may grow distant and insensitive to God's perfect and best will for your life. The adversary will appeal to your ego and pride. He will flatter you with anything and everything until he succeeds in getting you to act and behave independent of God's will. The only defense you can have is the presence, the indwelling of the Spirit of God. We should remember that Jesus said, John 16:7-11 (ESV),

It is to your advantage that I go away, for if I do not go away, the Helper will not come to you. But if I go, I will send him to you. And when he comes, he will convict the world concerning sin and righteousness and judgment: concerning sin, because they do not believe in me; concerning righteousness, because I go to the Father, and you will see me no longer; concerning judgment, because the ruler of this world is judged.

The presence and indwelling of the Holy Spirit's specific task is to bring conviction based upon the verities of God.

A fourth emphasis of Wiersbe's book was touched upon when Satan connived his way into the life and home of Job. The adversary is skilled at stating and evoking accusations. In the process, he targets the individual's heart and conscience. His ambition is to weaken and destroy. It is the similar identity of the thief mentioned by Jesus in John 10:10-13 (ESV),

The thief comes only to steal and kill and destroy. I came that they may have life and have it abundantly. I am the good shepherd. The good shepherd lays down his life for the sheep. He who is a hired hand and not a shepherd, who does not own the sheep, sees the wolf coming and leaves the sheep and flees, and the wolf snatches them and scatters them. He flees because he is a hired hand and cares nothing for the sheep.

The thief and Satan have in common their disregard for the sheep of God. They are bent on scattering and maiming God's flock and heritage. The source of safety and deliverance is in The Good Shepherd who is ready and willing to die on behalf of the sheep. When Peter wrote to the flock of God that was being persecuted and scattered, First Peter 1:13-21, he wanted them to maintain their focus on the Living God. He wrote,

> *Prepare your minds for action. Be sober-minded. Set your hope fully on the grace to be given you at the revelation of Jesus Christ...just as He who called you is holy, so be holy in all you do, for it is written: Be holy, because I am holy. Since you call on a Father who judges each man's work impartially, live your lives in reverent fear during your temporary stay on earth...Through Him you believe in God, who raised Him from the dead and glorified Him; and so your faith and hope are in God.*

Peter added the most suitable behavior that is to be common for the flock of God. A brief outline of it is given in First Peter 5:6-11,

> *Humble yourselves, therefore, under God's mighty hand, so that in due time He may exalt you. Cast all your anxiety on Him, because He cares for you. Be sober-minded and alert. Your adversary the devil prowls around like a roaring lion, seeking someone to devour. Resist him, standing firm in your faith and in the knowledge that your brothers throughout the world are undergoing the same kinds of suffering. And after you have suffered for a little while, the God of all grace, who has called you to His eternal glory in Christ, will Himself restore you, secure you, strengthen you, and establish you. To Him be the power forever and ever. Amen.*

This is the life you have been redeemed by Christ to live. How are you doing? Are you realizing and experiencing the full measure of unchained expectancy? If not, make the necessary changes in your life's preferences and embrace the teaching of God's Word.

Just this thought about the adversary. He knows he is a defeated foe. He knows his destiny and end. He continues to accuse the saints because that is his remaining desperate purpose. The scene described in Revelation 12:10-12 (ESV) is typical about him,

> *And I heard a loud voice in heaven, saying, Now the salvation and the power and the kingdom of our God and the authority of his Christ have come, for the accuser of our brothers has been thrown down, who accuses them day and night before our God. And they have conquered him by the blood of the Lamb and by the word of their testimony, for they loved not their lives even unto death. Therefore, rejoice, O heavens and you who dwell in them! But woe to you, O earth and sea, for the devil has come down to you in great wrath, because he knows that his time is short!*

The time of accusing God's people day and night is coming to end. The adversary knows that his time is short. Try as hard as he may, he will soon be bound in chains and cast into the lake of fire for the rest of eternity. Revelation 20:10-20 reminds God's people about their enemy,

> *The devil who had deceived them was thrown into the lake of fire and sulfur where the beast and the false prophet were, and they will be tormented day and night forever and ever. Then I saw a great white throne and him who was seated on it. From his presence earth and sky fled away, and no place was found for them. And I saw the dead, great and small, standing before the throne, and books were opened. Then another book was opened, which is the book of life. And the dead were judged by what was written in the books, according to what they had done. And the sea gave up the dead who were in it, Death and Hades gave up the dead who were in them, and they were*

> *judged, each one of them, according to what they had done. Then Death and Hades were thrown into the lake of fire. This is the second death, the lake of fire. And if anyone's name was not found written in the book of life, he was thrown into the lake of fire.*

The final day will come when no one expects it. It could be today or tomorrow; it could be sooner or later. Jesus stated, John 14:1-3, "I will come again and receive you unto myself, so that where I am, you will be also." Until that moment comes to pass, we can and should offer the prayer in Revelation 20:19-20 (ESV), "He who testifies to these things says, Surely I am coming soon. Amen. Come, Lord Jesus!"

Are you prepared for His coming? On what do you base your hope and confidence of entering God's heaven? Is it based upon who you are and what you have done or on Jesus Christ and who He is and what He has done? Are you able to personalize Ephesians 1:7-8, In Jesus Christ, I have redemption through His blood, the forgiveness of my sins and trespasses, according to the riches of His grace, which He lavished upon me"? If this is your valid testimony and witness, it signifies that you have been unchained and set free indeed in Jesus Christ.

Redeemed, how I love to proclaim it!
Redeemed by the blood of the Lamb;
Redeemed through His infinite mercy,
His child and forever I am.
Fanny Crosby

4. Prayer Perspective

Praying at all times in the Spirit, with all prayer and supplication. To that end keep alert with all perseverance, making supplication for all the saints, and also for me, that words may be given to me in opening my mouth boldly to proclaim the mystery of the gospel, for which I am an ambassador in chains, that I may declare it boldly, as I ought to speak.

Ephesians 6:18-20 (ESV)

The best way to maintain and preserve unchained expectations in the spiritual life is when prayer is frequent and comprehensive. On the Christian Apologetics and Research Ministry webpage, Matt Slick has addressed the subject, What Is Prayer? His initial answer is:

> *Prayer is the practice of the presence of God. It is the place where pride is abandoned, hope is lifted, and supplication is made. Prayer is the place of admitting our need, of adopting humility, and claiming dependence upon God. Prayer is the needful practice of the Christian. Prayer is the exercise of faith and hope. Prayer is the privilege of touching the heart of the Father through the Son of God, Jesus our Lord.*

The Westminster Shorter Catechism definition for prayer is,

> *Prayer is an offering up of our desires unto God for things agreeable to his will, in the name of Christ, with confession of our sins, and thankful acknowledgment of his mercies.*

Midway through the Sermon on the Mount, Jesus gives a guideline about effective and comprehensive prayer. While it is a beautifully worded prayer, Jesus never intended it to become a regular ritual in a local church worship service. It is a model for prayer rather than being a prayer that has become part of a ritual recited during each worship service. There is a focus for the prayer and that should serve as a guideline for the times when one prays. In Luke's account, we note (Luke 11:1 ESV), "Now Jesus was praying in a certain place, and when he finished, one of his disciples said to him, Lord, teach us to pray, as John taught his disciples."

A meaningful Hymn echoes the words of the disciples. We would do well to make it a part of our approach as we come before the Lord. When Peggy and I were married, this was used as the prayer hymn. The singular words were changed to plural (Teach US to pray…This is OUR heart-cry; WE long to know Thy will and Thy way). The original words are:

Teach me to pray, Lord, teach me to pray;
This is my heart-cry day unto day;
I long to know Thy will and Thy way;
Teach me to pray, Lord, teach me to pray.

For the purposes of this chapter, the Lord's Prayer will be personalized. The model prayer teaches us several important principles for prayer. The prayer begins with "Our Father" and is more meaningful when it conveys the idea of relationship, "My Father." It a personal relationship with Jesus Christ as Savior and Lord. It rests upon the words of Jesus Christ in John 10:30, "I and the Father are one."

The second part of the model prayer takes note of the place where "My Father" has been, is now and always will be - in heaven. One significant reason for noting this pertains to the words of Jesus Christ when he was speaking to His disciples about His departure from this earth. In John 14:1-3 (NASB). He said to them,

Do not let your heart be troubled; believe in God, believe also in Me. In My Father's house (heaven) are many dwelling places; if it were not so, I would have told you; for I go to prepare a place for you. If I go and prepare a place for you, I will come again and receive you to Myself, that where I am, there you may be also.

The disciples needed to know that there would be no political earthly kingdom. Jesus makes this clear as he assured them that they will reign with Him one day in the heavenly kingdom that is prepared for all who hear His voice and follow Him.

The next section of the model prayer emphasizes the important approach as one comes to God in prayer. This section directs us to focus completely upon our God in worship and adoration. It is recognition of His complete control of His world and our lives. Anne Graham Lotz has written a book on the subject of prayer. It is titled, The Daniel Prayer: Prayer That Moves Heaven and Changes Nations. On her Facebook entry, May 10, 2016, she wrote:

Years ago, I adopted the habit of beginning virtually every prayer with worship. I try to think of the specific attributes of His character relevant to my prayer. If I'm burdened for my children, I address Him as my Heavenly Father, worshipping Him as a parent who is supremely patient, loving, good, yet has children that are not perfect.

If I'm hurt and wounded, I address Him as the One who was wounded for my transgressions, who understands the feelings of my pain and who has promised to heal my broken heart. This simple exercise of putting my focus on who God is helps put my prayer into perspective. Refocus your prayers. When you

> *pray, focus singularly and intimately on God and on your conversation with Him!*

The three significant worship parts of the prayer are: Your name is hallowed (holy and sacred); Your kingdom come (consistent with Revelation 22:20, "He who testifies to these things says, Yes, I am coming soon. Amen. Come, Lord Jesus"); and Your will be done on earth as it is in heaven. It should be very clear that the initial focus in prayer is upon the triune God and the personal need to worship and adore Him. His followers are sometimes mistaken as they think of spiritual things in terms of themselves rather than in terms of the triune God. There is great validity and meaningfulness in the thought that it is not about you but it is all about Him.

As the prayer reaches its concluding thoughts, there are three phrases that are vital to the well-being of a child of God. They are – forgive me, lead me and deliver me. This section of the prayer deals with practical needs and interpersonal relationships. There are three basic parts to this section as well. The summary consists of the reality for daily needs to be met. It is with complete confidence that one comes before the Heavenly Father and prays give me today my daily bread. It is trusting in the God who promised in Matthew 6:31-33 (Personalized),

> *So do not worry, saying: What shall I eat? or What shall I drink? or What shall I wear? For the pagans run after all these things, and my heavenly Father knows that I need them. But if I seek first his kingdom and his righteousness, all these things will be given to me as well.*

These reassuring promises are often conveyed elsewhere in Scripture. Psalm 23:1, The Lord is my Shepherd, I shall not want." Someone paraphrased that into a testimony of God's goodness and benevolence by saying, "Because the

Lord is my Shepherd, I have everything that I need." Another verse that reminds us of God's sufficiency is Second Corinthians 9:8, "And God is able to make all grace abound to you, so that in all things, at all times, having all that you need, you will abound in every good work." Additionally, Philippians 4:19 (NLT) emphasizes: "And this same God who takes care of me will supply all my needs from his glorious riches, which have been given to me in Christ Jesus."

A very crucial and definitive petition in the model prayer focuses on the subject of forgiveness. It requires one to be both circumspect and transparent when the words prayed are, forgive me my debts (sins, trespasses) as I forgive anyone or everyone who has impacted my life as a debtor (sinned or trespassed against me). These words require reflection and meditation so that we do not gloss over the great need for my personal commitment to face my need to pray frequently - forgive me my debts (my sins. Also, sins are construed as debts as not rendering to God His due). It moves to and includes "As I also have forgiven my debtors (those who have sinned against me in some way, at some time). This area of forgiveness is crucial and very sobering because Jesus went on to teach (Verses 14-15),

> *For if you forgive other people when they sin against you, your heavenly Father will also forgive you. But if you do not forgive others their sins, your Father will not forgive your sins.*

There is no wiggle room for my personal interpretations, rationalizations or compromises. I either have a spirit of forgiveness and act upon it, or I ignore this obligation with the belief that I am exempt from its complete application. A person who lacks the desire to forgive places himself in the category of the non-believer. Paul also states a reason for the need to forgive when he wrote in Ephesians 4:30-32 (ESV),

And do not grieve the Holy Spirit of God, by whom you were sealed for the day of redemption. Let all bitterness and wrath and anger and clamor and slander be put away from you, along with all malice. Be kind to one another, tenderhearted, forgiving one another, as God in Christ forgave you.

The lesson taught is an obvious one. Along with all of the things listed that grieve the Holy Spirit of God, forgiving one another in a similar way by which Jesus Christ forgave you is included. This may be the most difficult part of the model prayer for most professing Christians. It is too easy to bear a grudge (a feeling of ill will or resentment) against another or to be angry toward someone who is disliked or disdained. This was one of the basic commands the children of Israel were expected to obey and implement. Leviticus 19:17-18 indicates in very clear terms:

You shall not hate your brother in your heart, but you shall reason frankly with your neighbor, lest you incur sin because of him. You shall not take vengeance or bear a grudge against the sons of your own people, but you shall love your neighbor as yourself: I am the Lord.

The importance and seriousness of this principle is that all sin, trespass or grudge-bearing is in direct violation of that which the Lord Himself has instituted. Violation of the command is an offense against the Lord who issued the directive.

The third personal emphasis is seen in the words "Lead me" and "Deliver me." These words are purposeful, intentional and echo Psalm 23:2-3, "He leads me beside still waters. He restores my soul. He leads me in paths of righteousness for his name's sake." In Psalm 23:4, "Even though I walk through the valley of the shadow of death, I will fear no evil, for you are with me" could be paraphrased that the Lord faithfully delivers me from the shadow of death and the lurking evil that is so common in the culture. Jesus wanted His followers to be dependent upon Him as they prayed: "Lead me not into temptation, but deliver me from the evil one."

Peter captured the force of these words when he wrote to those who were being persecuted and scattered in the first century. As was indicated earlier, Peter wrote to the believers (First Peter 5:6-9 - ESV) and to remind us all:

> *Humble yourselves, therefore, under the mighty hand of God so that at the proper time he may exalt you, casting all your anxieties on him, because he cares for you. Be sober-minded; be watchful. Your adversary the devil prowls around like a roaring lion, seeking someone to devour. Resist him, firm in your faith, knowing that the same kinds of suffering are being experienced by your brotherhood throughout the world.*

The evil one is seeking someone to devour. To gain an advantage over the evil one requires a particular discipline. It begins by being humble under the mighty hand of God. It requires one to be sober-minded and watchful for "the roaring lion" who is stalking and seeking someone to injure and devour. There is no special privilege afforded the child of God who is to be committed to resisting the adversary and to be unwavering in faith.

Matthew's version of the model prayer and Luke's version differ slightly at the conclusion of the prayer. Matthew includes a Benediction. It declares to the Heavenly Father: "Yours is the kingdom, power and glory forever." Prayer is effective because the kingdom belongs to the heavenly Father. There is no event or circumstance that can circumvent this fact. The evil one would love to have the child of God think and believe otherwise but that needs to be understood in terms of his subterfuge and deceit. Prayer is also effective because the heavenly Father is omnipotent (all-powerful). There is nothing that can restrain or prevent God from accomplishing all His will and purpose for His people and His universe. The last expression in the prayer is focused upon the glory of the heavenly Father. A reminder of this truth is shared with God's people in First Corinthians 1:26-31 (ESV),

> *For consider your calling, brethren, that there were not many wise according to the flesh, not many mighty, not many noble; but God has chosen the foolish things of the world to shame the wise, and God has chosen the weak things of the world to shame the things which are strong, and the base things of the world and the despised God has chosen, the things that are not, so that He may nullify the things that are, so that no man may boast before God. But by His doing you are in Christ Jesus, who became to us wisdom from God, and righteousness and sanctification, and redemption, so that, just as it is written, let him who boasts, boast in the Lord.*

The King James version translates verse 21, "He that glorieth, let him glory in the Lord." The reason is that all honor, praise and glory belong to the heavenly Father. The glory belongs to the Creator and not to anyone or anything that was created. There are times when the glory of the Lord is negated in the culture or taken matter-of-factly. When the Children of Israel were being delivered from Egypt, it was the glory of the Lord that led and protected them. If they neglected the presence and glory of the Lord, they would've been stalled in the desert and never reached the Promised Land.

How important is the glory of the Lord to us? Are we cognizant of it representing the presence of the Lord in the midst of His people? When was the last time you experienced the presence of the glory of the Lord in a local Church Worship Service? What does it literally mean when the church rises to sing either the Gloria Patri or the Doxology? Is it a weekly ritual in the worship service or does it represent that which is real for us?

There is a very dramatic scene in Ezekiel 9 through 11 (ESV) as the glory of the Lord begins to leave the Temple and the nation. The primary question is whether or not it matters to the majority of the people if the glory of the Lord is in their midst and surrounding them. Does it matter to you? Why?

Note the following progression as the glory of the Lord departs. The first stage of the departure is recorded in Ezekiel 9:3-5 (ESV), "Now the glory of the God of Israel went up from above the cherubim, where it had been, and moved to the threshold of the temple." The Almighty God has observed the sins of the people and their defiance toward Him and His purposes for the nation. The text adds,

> *Then the Lord called to the man clothed in linen who had the writing kit at his side and said to him: Go throughout the city of Jerusalem and put a mark on the foreheads of those who grieve and lament over all the detestable things that are done in it.*

The problem is the absence of grief and lamenting. For an indifferent and self-seeking people, the things of God had become irrelevant. If there was any grieving, it was God because of the behavior of His people. If there was any lamenting, it was God because of the hardness that had developed in the heart of His people. If we think that God doesn't grieve because of the sins of the people, recall what He said in Genesis 6:6 (ESV): "And the Lord regretted that he had made man on the earth, and it grieved Him to his heart."

God's indignation because of the sins of the nation and His people leads to the next stage of God's glory departing, Ezekiel 10:3-5 (ESV):

> *Now the cherubim were standing on the south side of the house, when the man went in, and a cloud filled the inner court. And the glory of the Lord went up from the cherub to the threshold of the house, and the house was filled with the cloud, and the court was filled with the brightness of the glory of the Lord. And the sound of the wings of the cherubim was heard as far as the outer court, like the voice of God Almighty when he speaks.*

Can you begin to sense the decibel volume that accompanied the sound of the wings of the cherubim? Ezekiel records that it was like the voice of God Almighty when He speaks. Do you imagine that the voice of Almighty God was a whisper or more like the roaring of thunder? It would've been loud and heard by anyone who was interested in listening. The sadness to this scene is that no one evidenced care or concern. No one stepped forward to repent. No one cried out to Almighty God that He remain in the midst of the Temple and nation. Everyone went about their regular routine with little or no thought about God. David penned the words of Psalm 9:15-17 (ESV) describing the plight of a nation of people who have ignored or become indifferent toward God. He wrote:

> *The nations have sunk in the pit that they made...The Lord has made himself known; he has executed judgment; the wicked are snared in the work of their own hands. The wicked shall return to Sheol (Hell), and all the nations that forget God.*

Ezekiel 10:18-19, speaks of another stage of the departure of the glory of God.

> *Then the glory of the Lord went out from the threshold of the house and stood over the cherubim. And the cherubim lifted up their wings and mounted up from the earth before my eyes as they went out...And they stood at the entrance of the east gate of the house of the Lord, and the glory of the God of Israel was over them.*

The glory of the Lord has moved from the Holy of Holies and the Temple. The sound and sight should've been recognized. However, everyone continued with their normal activities and no attention was given to this dramatic scene and event. A matter-of-factness prevailed and any seriousness about Almighty God was not present or expressed. The lack of any response on the part of the people indicates there was a dulling of the mind and heart toward spiritual things; a searing of the conscience regarding foundational principles, core values and moral standards and a practical atheism prevailing. The secular had been embraced rather than the spiritual.

The last vision of the glory of Almighty God departing appears in Ezekiel 11:22-23 (ESV):

> *Then the cherubim lifted up their wings... and the glory of the God of Israel was over them. And the glory of the Lord went up from the midst of the city and stood on the mountain that is on the east side of the city.*

With all of this movement of the glory of Almighty God and the accompanying sound of the angel's wings, will anyone pay some attention to Almighty God before it is too late? Will anyone plead with God to remain? Will there be indication of conviction among the people that will cause them to repent and return to the Lord? The glory of Almighty God is over the mountain. It is visible for the human eye to behold. The thunderous sound that accompanied this movement could be heard. The sad and devastating result is that no one observed, no one listened, no one paid any attention, no one seemed to care about their spiritual plight or the absence of the presence of God in their midst. The end had been reached by Almighty God and His reserved judgment would now become their reality. Much like the flood in Noah's day, or the fiery end of Sodom and Gomorrah in Abraham and Lot's Day, so it is at this juncture for the people who have forgotten and ignored God. The threshold has been crossed and they are now on the slippery slope of despair, confusion and being cast into the abyss of darkness.

The theme, purpose and vision for us is encapsulated in the words: "The best way to maintain and preserve unchained expectations in the spiritual life is where prayer is frequent and comprehensive." Are you maintaining a personal and intimate relationship with the Heavenly Father? If so, you have limitless and unchained expectancy. If not, then your plight will be the same as in previous generations when people ignored and were indifferent to Almighty God and His Word.

In 1936, J. Edwin Orr penned the words that can be used as and when we begin to pray. Each of us should emphasize as we sing and pray:

Search ME, O God, And know MY heart today;
Try ME, O Savior, Know MY thoughts, I pray.
See if there be Some wicked way in ME;
Cleanse ME from every sin And set ME free.

In most church communion services, there is a reminder shared prior to one's partaking of the sacrament of the Lord's Supper. It is traditional for First Corinthians 11:23-32 to be read and a prayer of confession to be offered. The statement that underscores this practice is in verses 28-29,

> *Each one must examine himself before he eats of the bread and drinks of the cup. For anyone who eats and*

drinks without recognizing the body eats and drinks judgment on himself.

As the personal searching of one's soul, heart and life is in process, Psalm 19:12-14 should also be a prominent part of one's prayer:

Who can discern his errors? Declare me innocent from hidden faults. Keep back your servant also from presumptuous sins; let them not have dominion over me! Then I shall be blameless, and innocent of great transgression. Let the words of my mouth and the meditation of my heart be acceptable in your sight, O Lord, my rock and my redeemer.

A definitive and cautionary word is given in Numbers 15:30-31(NLT)

But those who brazenly violate the Lord's will, whether native-born Israelites or foreigners, have blasphemed the Lord, and they must be cut off from the community. Since they have treated the Lord's word with contempt and deliberately disobeyed his command, they must be completely cut off and suffer the punishment for their guilt.

All of this must be more than a tradition or ritual. It is dealing with the likelihood of unconfessed sin and one's sense of personal unworthiness. It causes one to reflect upon the attitude and practices one has toward others. It should cause one to reflect upon Ephesians 4:30-32 and those things that grieve the Holy Spirit of God. This enables one to cross the threshold into a greater sense of unchained expectancy for the soul that has been set free indeed by Jesus Christ.

5. Prayer Implementation

You also must help us by prayer, so that many will give thanks on our behalf for the blessing granted us through the prayers of many. First of all, then, I urge that supplications, prayers, intercessions, and thanksgivings be made for all people, for kings and all who are in high positions, that we may lead a peaceful and quiet life, godly and dignified in every way.

Second Corinthians 1:11 and First Timothy 2:1-2

A great challenge for the people of God is the discipline to pray and to maintain an attitude of prayer. There are many situations that can easily distract from purposeful and transparent prayer. We should always want to come before the Heavenly Father with unchained expectations. There is a reason that Jesus instructed a simple solution regarding prayer in Matthew 6:5-6 (NASB),

> *When you pray, you are not to be like the hypocrites; for they love to stand and pray in the synagogues and on the street corners so that they may be seen by men. Truly I say to you, they have their reward in full. But you, when you pray, go into your inner room, close your door and pray to your Father who is in secret, and your Father who sees what is done in secret will reward you.*

It is obvious that the average professing Christian has areas where improvement and reordering of priorities is necessary. Our lives can so easily become filled with clutter. Anne Graham Lotz shared an observation on Facebook regarding Prayer,

> *Many people today find that their prayers don't 'work.' And like a broken cell phone, DVD player, or TV remote, they throw prayer out as unnecessary 'clutter' in their busy lives…Prayer does work, sometimes the 'pray-ers' don't. This statement encapsulates the area for conscious effort on our part to repair it quickly. We need to enter the alone place that is free from distraction. Once we do, we can have precious and purposeful moments in conversation with the Heavenly Father. It will be a time for worship of Him; exalting and magnifying His name; giving Him glory, reverence and honor.*

The Lord Jesus Christ gave us instruction in the manner and discipline by which we are to approach the heavenly Father. There is a three-step formulation that is in the present active tense, Matthew 7:7-11 (NASB),

> *Ask, and it will be given to you; seek, and you will find; knock, and it will be opened to you. For everyone who asks receives, and he who seeks finds, and to him who knocks it will be opened. Or what man is there among you who, when his son asks for a loaf, will give him a stone? Or if he asks for a fish, he will not give him a snake, will he? If you then, being evil, know how to give good gifts to your children, how much more will your Father who is in heaven give what is good to those who ask Him!*

The passage begins with the direction to "ask" and concludes with the summation "ask Him." The force of the present active tense is for a person of faith to know one is granted direction to (a) keep on asking, (b) keep on seeking and (c) keep on knocking. Jesus assures us that as we keep on asking, we will receive; as we keep on seeking, we will find and as we keep on knocking, the door of blessing will be opened. It is a continuous action of praying at all times and on all occasions for all things. Paul summed it with a three-word directive that should be common to God's people (First Thessalonians 5:17, NASB), "Pray without ceasing." In the NLT, the statement is very clear, "Never stop praying."

Jesus taught this same principle in His parable on prayer in Luke 18:1-8 (NASB). While the section begins with prayer, the question at the end is piercing, "When the Son of Man comes, will He find faith on the earth?" The parable illustrates the basic principle of "keep on asking and you will keep on receiving" that which is good and in accord with God's will for you. It also includes the place for persistence in one's prayer focus and need.

> *Now He (Jesus) was telling them a parable to show that at all times they ought to pray and not to lose heart, saying, In a certain city there was a judge who did not fear God and did not respect man. There was a widow in that city, and she kept coming to him, saying, Give me legal protection from my opponent. For a while he was unwilling; but afterward he said to himself, Even though I do not fear God nor respect man, yet because this widow bothers me, I will give her legal protection, otherwise by continually coming she will wear me out. And the Lord said, Hear what the unrighteous judge said; now, will not God bring about justice for His elect who cry to Him day and night, and will He delay long over them? I tell you that He will bring about justice for them quickly. However, when the Son of Man comes, will He find faith on the earth?*

The widow was in a desperate situation and she came to the one who could legally assist her. Regardless of his initial dismissal of her, with discipline and persistence, she came and presented her case. The reluctant judge heeded and acted upon her request. His reasoning for doing so is recorded as, "Even though I do not fear God nor respect man, yet because this widow bothers me, I will give her legal protection, otherwise by continually coming she will wear me out." He did not want to deal with her persistence and viewed her coming as that which bothered him. He is becoming frustrated with her persistence and yielded to her request for a self-serving reason, "otherwise by continually coming she will wear me out."

Additional thoughts about the ask, seek, knock formulation for prayer has these definitive words that undergird the implementation of keep on asking, keep on seeking and keep on knocking. Earlier in the Sermon on the Mount, Jesus shared with His followers the reasons why they should not worry or be anxious about the temporal needs of life. He wanted to convey that you as an individual follower are important to Him. He wants us to be free from anxieties and the undue concerns for the temporal matters of life. In Matthew 6:25-34, He taught,

> *I say to you, do not be worried about your life, as to what you will eat or what you will drink; nor for your body, as to what you will put on. Is not life more than food, and the body more than clothing? Look at the birds of the air, that they do not sow, nor reap nor gather into barns, and yet your heavenly Father feeds them. Are you not worth much more than they? And who of you by being worried can add a single hour to his life? And why are you worried about clothing? Observe how the lilies of the field grow; they do not toil nor do they spin, yet I say to you that not even Solomon in all his glory clothed himself like one of these. But if God so clothes the grass of the field, which is alive today and tomorrow is thrown into the furnace, will He not much more clothe you? You of little faith! Do not worry then, saying, What will we eat? or What will we drink? or What will we wear for*

clothing? For the Gentiles eagerly seek all these things; for your heavenly Father knows that you need all these things. But seek first His kingdom and His righteousness, and all these things will be added to you. So do not worry about tomorrow; for tomorrow will care for itself.

As and when we pray, we usually have a checklist of things we would like to have God provide and do. We consume considerable prayer time by mentioning these things repeatedly. It should be reassuring for us to remember that God is never ignorant about who we are, where we are or what we need. Jesus underscores the words above, "Your heavenly Father knows that you need all these things. But seek first His kingdom and His righteousness, and all these things will be added to you."

Our God is an awesome and omniscient (all-knowing) God. He knows every detail of our lives. Additionally, He is also the omnipotent (all powerful) God who is unlimited in what He can do for you. It serves one well to remember a prayer offered by Paul in Ephesians 3:20-21 (NASB),

Now to Him who is able to do far more abundantly beyond all that we ask or think, according to the power that works within us, to Him be the glory in the church and in Christ Jesus to all generations forever and ever. Amen." Just pause for a moment and weigh the magnitude of the phrase "according to the power that works within us." He is also more than able to surpass our unchained expectations because He "is able to do far more abundantly beyond all that we ask or think (imagine).

Does the Almighty God hear our prayers when we offer them to Him? The answer is, Yes! Why is it that some of our prayers seem to be unanswered? What is the problem that prevents the answer we seek from God?

One possibility is personal motivation. In James 4:2-3 (NASB), the veneer is peeled away and a cause is stated as, "You do not have because you do not ask. You ask and do not receive, because you ask with wrong motives, so that you may spend it on your pleasures." What is your motivation when you pray? Is it possible that one's prayer life has become a device to selfishly get and gain personally? Is it possible that spiritual pride could be an issue in one's life? Are your prayers couched in the understanding of "not my will, but Your will, be done"?

Another possibility is the measure of intensity with which one prays. One of the vital areas that is becoming foreign to the twenty-first century Church is prayer accompanied with purposeful fasting. Interestingly, while Jesus does not attach fasting to the model prayer in Matthew 6:9-13, He does mention the proper way for His followers who utilize fasting for a specific purpose. Matthew 6:16-18 (NASB), Jesus makes an assumption when He said,

> *Whenever you fast, do not put on a gloomy face as the hypocrites do, for they neglect their appearance so that they will be noticed by men when they are fasting. Truly I say to you, they have their reward in full. But you, when you fast, anoint your head and wash your face so that your fasting will not be noticed by men, but by your Father who is in secret; and your Father who sees what is done in secret will reward you.*

There is an occasion in Matthew 17:14-21 (NASB) when a man approached Jesus about his son whom he identified as a lunatic (or demoniac). He indicates that he had brought his son to the disciples but they were unable to deal with the son's issue. Jesus almost sounds annoyed as he said,

You unbelieving and perverted generation, how long shall I be with you? How long shall I put up with you? Bring him here to Me. And Jesus rebuked him, and the demon came out of him, and the boy was cured at once.

What was the determining factor at this point? What is the determining factor for the biblical Christian today? The disciples have that concern as well, Matthew 17:19-21 (NASB),

Then the disciples came to Jesus privately and said: Why could we not drive it out? And He said to them: Because of the littleness of your faith; for truly I say to you, if you have faith the size of a mustard seed, you will say to this mountain, move from here to there, and it will move; and nothing will be impossible to you. But this kind does not go out except by prayer and fasting.

John Calvin's Commentary on The Gospel of Matthew shares the following (Pages 492-496):

By this expression, Jesus Christ reproved the negligence of certain persons, in order to inform them that it was not an ordinary faith which was required; for otherwise they might have replied that they were not altogether destitute of faith. The meaning therefore is, that it is not every kind of faith that will suffice, when we have to enter into a serious conflict with Satan, but that vigorous efforts are indispensably necessary. For the weakness of faith, he prescribes prayer as a remedy, to which he adds fasting by way of an auxiliary...You have to deal with a powerful adversary, who will not yield till the battle has been fought out. Your faith must therefore be excited by prayer, and as you are slow and languid in prayer, you must resort to fasting as an assistance.

Several years ago, a denomination of which I was a part called the churches and people to a Day of Prayer and Fasting for specific needs. As the Day for Prayer and Fasting approached, Pastors were urged to share with their respective congregations the purpose and practice of fasting. In several instances, people began to raise questions about it. They also suggested personal health issues that would prevent it. There were pockets of resistance to the idea and principle of fasting. I suspect Jesus might've been annoyed about the hesitancy by several people to implement a teaching that He stated was vital and his prescription regarding how it should be practiced. Even though it was a challenge to a new experience in spiritual exercise, several participated and were appreciative of being asked to do so.

Perhaps the contemporary church is in the same state as the exiles during the days of Ezra and Nehemiah. Ezra's Prayer of Confession, Ezra 9:4-5 (NASB) is very striking,

> *Then everyone who trembled at the words of the God of Israel on account of the unfaithfulness of the exiles gathered to me, and I sat appalled until the evening offering. But at the evening offering I arose from my humiliation, even with my garment and my robe torn, I fell on my knees and stretched out my hands to the Lord my God; and I said, O my God, I am ashamed and embarrassed to lift up my face to You, my God, for our iniquities have risen above our heads and our guilt has grown even to the heavens.*

Where is the sense of humiliation before God in the twenty-first century Church? Where is the contrition for the sins of omission and commission? Whatever happened to repentance before a Holy God? When did we stop taking a serious God seriously?

An additional consideration is that we should never think about traditional or liturgical prayers as some form of spiritual magic if we recite the prayer in a certain way. Before teaching a lesson about prayer and sharing a model prayer form and format with the disciples, Jesus states in Matthew 6:7-8,

> *And when (as) you are praying, do not use meaningless repetition as the Gentiles (heathen) do, for they suppose that they will be heard for their many words. So do not be like them; for your Father knows what you need before you ask Him.*

An illustration of vain repetitions is given in First Kings 18:25-29 (NASB) when Elijah is in dialogue and contest with the Prophets of Baal,

> *So Elijah said to the prophets of Baal, Choose one ox for yourselves and prepare it first for you are many, and call on the name of your god, but put no fire under it. Then they took the ox which was given them and they prepared it and called on the name of Baal from morning until noon saying, O Baal, answer us. But there was no voice and no one answered. And they leaped about the altar which they made. It came about at noon, that Elijah mocked them and said, Call out with a loud voice, for he is a god; either he is occupied or gone aside, or is on a journey, or perhaps he is asleep and needs to be awakened. So they cried with a loud voice and cut themselves according to their custom with swords and lances until the blood gushed out on them. When midday was past, they raved until the time of the offering of the evening sacrifice; but there was no voice, no one answered, and no one paid attention.*

Vain repetitions always bring about a similar result: “there was no voice, no one answered, and no one paid attention.” There is a time and place for some forms of worship to be utilized. The concern is whether or not the words used in the form have any practical meaning in the immediate. Forms are not a religious magical formula.

The practical petitions to God are the best expression of unchained expectations. When Peter tried to walk on the water to Jesus, after he took his eyes off of Jesus and began to sink in the storm-tossed sea, his simple petition was: “Lord, help!”

The situation in Matthew 17 mentioned above, about a father’s concern for his lunatic son, Mark 9:23-24 underscores a very practical statement of faith and prayer, “Jesus said to him, If You can? All things are possible to him who believes. Immediately the boy’s father cried out and said, I do believe; help my unbelief.” More often than not, those who pray a simple form of prayer gain the satisfaction of God’s sense of their desperation and the immediacy of the need. It also serves as a preventative for one who might fall prey by dictating to God what and how He should do that which you think should be done.

On another occasion, a crowd was following Jesus and pressing around him. A woman with a persistent and desperate need for many years wants to have Jesus address her need. The crowd is dense but she manages to work her way through the crowd. She reaches out her hand toward Jesus and is able to touch the hem of His garment. Matthew 9:20-22 (NASB) records the event,

> *And a woman who had been suffering from a hemorrhage for twelve years, came up behind Him and touched the fringe of His cloak; for she was saying to herself, If I only touch His garment, I will get well. But Jesus turning and seeing her said, Daughter, take*

courage; your faith has made you well. At once the woman was made well.

By faith, she reached out to Jesus. By faith alone, Jesus made her well and whole. No form or ritual was needed. Her faith and confidence in the power of Jesus Christ was all she needed and was more than sufficient to meet her need.

How is it with you as you consider praying? Do you get all tangled up in forms, rituals and traditions? Or, do you come to the heavenly Father with unchained expectancy as you cast all your cares upon Him because you know He cares for you (First Peter 5:8)?

The idea of prayer implementation is to just do it. Just pray without ceasing! May God enrich and enhance your spiritual life as you pray and commune with your Heavenly Father. May the Lord unshackle you from everything that hinders your seeking Him with unchained expectancy.

6. Church Growth

It is necessary that of the men who have accompanied us all the time that the Lord Jesus went in and out among us, beginning with the baptism of John until the day that He was taken up from us, one of these must become a witness with us of His resurrection. So they put forward two men, Joseph called Barabbas (who was also called Justus), and Matthias. And they prayed and said, You, Lord, who know the hearts of all men, show which one of these two You have chosen to occupy this ministry and apostleship from which Judas turned aside to go to his own place. And they drew lots for them, and the lot fell to Matthias; and he was added to the eleven apostles.

Acts 1:21-26

The first act of the eleven after the ascension of Jesus Christ was to select a replacement for Judas Iscariot. It was determined it should be one who had witnessed the resurrection of Jesus Christ. Before anyone was selected, they prayed: "You, Lord, who know the hearts of all men, show which one of these two You have chosen to occupy this ministry and apostleship." The unchained expectancy of the Apostles was to go forward in the ministry entrusted to them by Jesus Christ. They took the commission, mandate and enabling power of Jesus Christ seriously. They were motivated by the words of Jesus to them, John 20:21-22 (NASB), "Peace be with you; as the Father has sent Me, I also send you. And when He had said this, He breathed on them and said to them, Receive the Holy Spirit." The words of Jesus in Matthew 28:18-20 (NASB) also resonated with the disciples,

Jesus spoke to them, saying: All authority (power) has been given to Me in heaven and on earth. Go

> *therefore and make disciples of all the nations, baptizing them in the name of the Father and the Son and the Holy Spirit, teaching them to observe all that I commanded you; and lo, I am with you always, even to the end of the age.*

Being challenged, motivated and empowered, they were ready to go anywhere, face any foe, meet any challenge, pay any price so that the Gospel of the Lord Jesus Christ would be declared to the countless numbers of people who needed to hear so they could believe. Despite the challenges before them, they were fearless as they represented Jesus Christ.

They recognized that the church to be birthed was intended to be the liberated enemy of "the god of this world" (Second Corinthians 4:4). We, the followers of Jesus Christ, are the guerrillas and the gadflies in the world. We are not bound by ecclesiastical forms, rituals or traditions. We are to be the insurgency in the rebel kingdom of "the prince of the power of the air" (Ephesians 2:2). We must fulfill our role with discipline and determination. We must not allow laxity or luxury to sidetrack us from the assignment given by Jesus Christ. We have been made aware of the enemy and his scheming. We have also been made aware of mission and mandate of the Savior, Jesus Christ. When I was a youth, a popular chorus that was sung at Bible conferences and camps was written by Alfred Smith, With Eternity's Values In View. The thrust of the lyrics was that each day's work was to have the priority of eternity in full view. The scales of heaven and hell was in one's hands with the outcome based upon the genuineness of one's work for Jesus with eternity's values in view!

In a very brief sketch of the Book of Acts, to adequately accomplish the assigned task we observe the significant role prayer had in the practical needs as they arose. In the Gospels, prayer is part of the spiritual life in all ministry that is done. It is mentioned specifically by Matthew ten times; by Mark twelve times; by Luke nineteen times and John five times. In The Book of Acts, Luke mentions the significance of prayer thirty-two times. After the Ascension of Jesus Christ (Acts 1:9-11), those who had witnessed it returned to Jerusalem and the upper room where they had been staying (Acts 1:12-13). We learn two things immediately about this upper room gathering in Acts 1:14, "They were all with one mind and they were continually devoting themselves to prayer." These two upper room principles are needed in personal lives as well as in the Church as it exists today. There is a drift away from being of one mind. Similarly, prayer can appear to be a religious thing we tack onto our Church agendas rather than a primary part of who and what we are. If the professing Christians could arrive at the one mind point and continually devote themselves to prayer, the result would be positive and remarkable. Do you ever long for a gathering of likeminded Biblical Christians in an upper room atmosphere and experience?

I remember fondly a family in a church startup who opened a room above their garage where we were able to have an upper room bible study and prayer time. There was a spirit of oneness and prayer was a central part of our gathering. Camaraderie (mutual trust and friendship among people who spend a lot of time together) resulted. It was a friendship and fellowship that does not often occur. It is sorely missed and is absent from several places where it should be present. It is a situation where people don't just talk religion but walk and practice true religion that is undefiled by the culture or personal biases. Do you belong to a Church or group where such camaraderie is both natural and present?

Some great servants of old wrote about the significant difference there must be in a Biblical Christian's life. One of them was Dr. A. W. Tozer (1897-1963), who preached a

Sermon on the subject, *Devotion To Things Holy* In which he stated:

> *Success is any field is costly, but the man who will pay the price can have it. The concert pianist must become a slave to his instrument; four hours, five hours each day he must sit at the keyboard. The scientist must live for his work. The philosopher must devote himself to thought, the scholar to his books. The price may seem excessively heavy, but there are some who consider the reward worthwhile. The laws of success operate also in the higher field of the soul. Spiritual greatness has its price. Eminence in the things of the Spirit demands a devotion to these things more complete than most of us are willing to give. But the law cannot be escaped. If we would be holy, we know the way; the law of holy living is before us. The prophets of the Old Testament, the apostles of the New and, more than all, the sublime teachings of Christ are there to tell us how to succeed.*

There is such a great need today for God's servants who will proclaim with clarity that God remains ready to feed the hungry soul who seeks for Him with all of one's heart. The one feeding the hungry soul is the one devoted to things holy. That's what He gives and that's what nourishes and fills the hungry soul.

There is a transitional period from Luke 24 to Acts 1. The Lord Jesus Christ has ascended into heaven but they recall He had remarked that He would not leave them as orphans. He indicated the Holy Spirit would come and be with them and empower them. In anticipation of that which Jesus taught in John 14 and 16, they gathered in the upper room where they prayed and waited. The remainder of Acts 1 has Peter assuming a leadership role and reaching a consensus of a replacement for Judas Iscariot who had betrayed the Lord Jesus Christ and afterwards committed suicide.

This group remained in the upper room until it became obvious the time was right to leave. As they emerged, they were completely different people of God. They were fearless. Gone were their doubts and denials. They had gained a new confidence and boldness. Even though they had experienced unchained expectancy, they had no idea how that would be carried out in and through them.

The Church today is so well organized and structured there seems to be little or no time allotted for the upper room times and experiences. Serious soul-searching is needed to determine if the purpose of a Church's existence is man or God-centered. One can only wonder whether or not the structured Church has inadvertently allowed for the quenching of the Holy Spirit (First Thessalonians 5:19, "Quench not the Spirit"). The Berean Study Bible translates the verse, "Do not extinguish the Spirit." Crowded schedules appear to be the enemy's tactic to prevent a contemporary upper room time alone with God and being in the presence of God.

After this spirit of oneness and devotion to prayer in the upper room, Acts 2 ushers in the day of Pentecost. Acts 2:1-4 (NASB) records: "When the day of Pentecost had come, they were all together in one place." The unexpected and unpredictable result was:

> *Suddenly there came from heaven a noise like a violent rushing wind, and it filled the whole house where they were sitting. And there appeared to them tongues as of fire distributing themselves, and they rested on each one of them. And they were all filled with the Holy Spirit and began to speak with other tongues, as the Spirit was giving them utterance.*

Just to be clear, "to speak with other tongues" is derived from the Greek word glossais. You can glean the sense of the actual meaning "utterance" and "other tongues" in this context by going to Acts 2:7-12 (NASB) where it is said,

They were amazed and astonished, saying, Why, are not all these who are speaking Galileans. And how is it that we each hear them in our own language to which we were born? We hear them in our own tongues speaking of the mighty deeds of God. And they all continued in amazement and great perplexity, saying to one another, What does this mean?

This text is clear that they were speaking the Word of God in known languages and dialects. The obvious purpose was to convey the Gospel to every tribe, tongue, nation and people. Since great numbers and representations of such people were present, the Holy Spirit enabled God's servants to communicate the Gospel so that everyone present, regardless of their language or dialect, could hear and understand the basic gospel message as stated by Jesus in John 8:31-36 (ESV),

So Jesus said to the Jews who had believed him, If you abide in my word, you are truly my disciples, and you will know the truth, and the truth will set you free...if the Son sets you free, you will be free indeed.

The word "indeed" is an adverb that means: "in fact, in reality, in truth." It conveys confirmation and amplifies the statement of fact that preceded it, If the Son shall make you free, you shall be free INDEED." This is part of what occurred as a result of the time spent together in prayer in the upper room.

Acts 2 also records the sermon preached by Peter on the day of Pentecost. It was dynamic, courageous, powerful and fearless. He began with reference to the prophet Joel, Acts 2:14-21 (NASB Selected),

But Peter, taking his stand with the eleven, raised his voice and declared to them: Men of Judea and all you who live in Jerusalem, let this be known to you and

give heed to my words...this is what was spoken of through the prophet Joel: and it shall be in the last days, God says, that I will pour forth of my Spirit on all mankind; and your sons and your daughters shall prophesy, and your young men shall see visions, and your old men shall dream dreams; even on my bond-slaves, both men and women, I will in those days pour forth of my spirit and they shall prophesy. and I will grant wonders in the sky above and signs on the earth below, blood, and fire, and vapor of smoke. the sun will be turned into darkness and the moon into blood, before the great and glorious day of the Lord shall come. and it shall be that everyone who calls on the name of the Lord will be saved.

Peter goes on to give an abbreviated summary about the life and purpose of Jesus Christ, Acts 2:22-24 (NASB),

Men of Israel, listen to these words: Jesus the Nazarene, a man attested to you by God with miracles and wonders and signs which God performed through Him in your midst, just as you yourselves know, this Man, delivered over by the predetermined plan and foreknowledge of God, you nailed to a cross by the hands of godless men and put Him to death. But God raised Him up again, putting an end to the agony of death, since it was impossible for Him to be held in its power.

The result was greater than anyone could have anticipated or expected. The Lord used ordinary men, who met in earnest in the Upper Room, in an extra-ordinary way on the day of Pentecost to accomplish His eternal purpose. Acts 2:37-41 (NASB) records the response to the words preached by Peter,

Now when they heard this, they were pierced to the heart, and said to Peter and the rest of the apostles,

Brethren, what shall we do?" Peter said to them: Repent, and each of you be baptized in the name of Jesus Christ for the forgiveness of your sins; and you will receive the gift of the Holy Spirit. For the promise is for you and your children and for all who are far off, as many as the Lord our God will call to Himself. And with many other words he solemnly testified and kept on exhorting them, saying, Be saved from this perverse generation! So then, those who had received his word were baptized; and that day there were added about three thousand souls.

It is important to note that when God's work is done in God's way and in God's timing it will always bring about God's result. Historically, there were unchained expectancy moments. One was known as the Haystack Prayer Meeting. A brief History documented by Global Ministries indicates the following as having occurred:

Five Williams College students met in the summer of 1806, in a grove of trees near the Hoosack River, then known as Sloan's Meadow, and debated the theology of missionary service. Their meeting was suddenly interrupted by a thunderstorm and the students: Samuel J. Mills, James Richards, Francis L. Robbins, Harvey Loomis, and Byram Green took shelter under a haystack until the sky cleared. The brevity of the shower, the strangeness of the place of refuge, and the peculiarity of their topic of prayer and conference all took hold of their imaginations and their memories. In 1808 the Haystack Prayer group and other Williams students began a group called The Brethren. This group was organized to effect, in the persons of its members, a mission to those who were not Christians. In 1812, the ABCFM (American Board Of Commissioners For Foreign Missions) sent its first missionaries to the Indian subcontinent. Samuel Mills became the Haystack person with the greatest influence on the modern mission movement. He played a role in the founding of the American Bible Society and the United Foreign Missionary Society.

(www.globalministries.org)

Another unique opportunity was the Fulton Street Prayer Meeting in New York City. Many sources reference this event but the original record of it was written and published in Christian Life Magazine. The following is copied from Knowing and Doing (A Teaching Quarterly for Discipleship of Heart and Mind),

> *It was exactly 12 noon on September 23, 1857. A tall, middle-aged former businessman climbed creaking stairs to the third story of an old church building in the heart of lower New York City. He entered an empty room, pulled out his pocket watch and sat down to wait. The placard outside read: Prayer Meeting from 12 to 1 o'clock—Stop 5, 10, or 20 minutes, or the whole hour, as your time admits. It looked like no one had the time. As the minutes ticked by, the solitary waiter wondered if it were all a mistake.*
>
> *He waited ten minutes, then ten more. The minute hand of his watch pointed to 12:30 when at last he heard a step on the stairs. One man came in, then another and another until there were six. After a few minutes of prayer, the meeting was dismissed with the decision that another meeting would be held the following Wednesday. That small meeting was in no way extraordinary. There was no great outpouring of the Spirit of God. Lanphier had no way of knowing that it was the beginning of a great national revival which would sweep an estimated one million persons into the kingdom of God.*

> *Within six months 10,000 businessmen (out of a population of 800,000) were gathering daily in New York City for prayer. In January 1858 there were at least twenty other prayer meetings going full tilt in the city. Many of them were sparked by the Young Men's Christian Association. Other cities had them too. By January of 1858 newspapers were sending reporters to cover the meetings. "The Progress of the Revival" became a standing news head. Remarkable cases of awakening were detailed at length. And there were many.*

Is the God of the upper room and the day of Pentecost still able to take ordinary people and use them in an extraordinary way today? If we came to Him openly and with unchained expectancy, would God be pleased to empower a new generation to reach the decadent culture of these days? I was moved and touched deeply by a note I received that asked the following question,

> *Where, O where is that upper room? I know only the Spirit can make it happen. But I grieve for my brothers and sisters here who are missing such fellowship and joy.*

How I wish I could answer the question about a location for an upper room gathering. It is obviously needed. Another question comes to my mind: Do we believe that we are currently empowered by the Lord to do His work in His way? If not, for what are waiting? Who will stand in the gap and represent the Lord amid the chaos and loss of spiritual direction here and now? This was a challenge spoken of in Ezekiel 22:23-31 (ESV). Some of the Words of the Lord to His servant about the times in which he is living include:

> *You are a land that is not cleansed or rained upon in the day of indignation. The conspiracy of her prophets*

in her midst is like a roaring lion tearing the prey; they have devoured human lives; they have taken treasure and precious things; they have made many widows in her midst. Her priests have done violence to my law and have profaned my holy things...they have disregarded my Sabbaths, so that I am profaned among them. Her princes in her midst are like wolves tearing the prey, shedding blood, destroying lives to get dishonest gain. And her prophets...seeing false visions and divining lies for them, saying: Thus says the Lord God, when the Lord has not spoken. The people of the land have practiced extortion and committed robbery. They have oppressed the poor and needy and have extorted from the sojourner without justice. And I sought for a man among them who should build up the wall and stand in the breach (stand in the gap) before me for the land, that I should not destroy it, but I found none. Therefore, I have poured out my indignation upon them. I have consumed them with the fire of my wrath. I have returned their way upon their heads, declares the Lord God.

Does any of this sound familiar? Does it serve as a critique for the day in which we are living? Is it possible that the Lord is seeking you to be that person? Are you willing to make yourself available to Him to go to any place, at any time, to do any work, at any cost?

Read the challenging words and call for commitment in Second Timothy 2:11-13 (NIV),

Here is a trustworthy saying: If we died with him, we will also live with him; if we endure, we will also reign with him. If we disown him, he will also disown us; if we are faithless, he remains faithful, for he cannot disown himself.

How will you respond to this challenge and call for commitment? Is unchained expectancy your reality? Is it visibly present anywhere today? Is there an upper room where people of one mind gather together, and pray with fervor and expectancy? If there was such a place, would you be a faithful participant? Those who have been unchained and been made free indeed by Jesus Christ should have time for such a place and time. As and when this occurs, there will also be the presence and power of the Lord Jesus Christ in the midst of His people. Be reminded and encouraged by the words in Second Peter 1:2-3,

> *Grace and peace be multiplied to you in the knowledge of God and of Jesus our Lord; seeing that His divine power has granted to us everything pertaining to life and godliness, through the true knowledge of Him who called us by His own glory and excellence.*

Church planting and growth should never be planned or seen as an organized mechanical effort. It is not the work or ingenuity of any man or group of people. It is accomplished by the work of the Holy Spirit working through ordinary people who have been unshackled and set free indeed. The Holy Spirit will enable them to accomplish that which is extraordinary by His power and for the glory of Christ alone. Are you eager for the Holy Spirit to work in and through you to accomplish God's work as it is done in God's way?

Thy way, not mine, O Lord,
However dark it be;
Lead me by Thine own hand,
Choose out the path for me.
Smooth let it be or rough,
It will be still the best;
Winding or straight, it leads
Right onward to Thy rest.

Words By: Horatius Bonar (1857)

7. My Transformation

I appeal to you therefore, brothers,-by the mercies of God, to present your bodies as a living sacrifice, holy and acceptable to God, which is your spiritual worship. Do not be conformed to this world, but be transformed by the renewal of your mind, that by testing you may discern what is the will of God, what is good and acceptable and perfect.

Romans 12:1-2 (ESV)

A perennial question is: How seriously do we take a serious God? When it comes to the application of God's Word in our daily lives, do we intentionally obey it or accidentally stumble into complying with God's values? When consideration is given to whether or not our choices are more in keeping with conformity to the culture and world rather than being transformed by the spiritual renewal of mind and will to be brought into conformity to God's will, some might pause and respond with a "Huh?". I have often thought about: Why do people own a Bible? Why do they desire an identity with some religious group or visible Church? Why do some attend a visible Church (if only occasionally)? On a broader scale, why are mega-churches seemingly popular and growing? As we consider the diminishing religious influence in our culture and world today, what is the basis and determinative factor for moral values and ethical choices? How does a culture and society become what it is? Are these, and other areas of life, a result of intentional choices or accidental occurrences?

The personal commitment is for one to be different so that he can make a difference in the lives of others. It will necessitate transformational and intentional living and a level of transparency with others of like precious faith. Sometimes when one shares his personal flaws or foibles with those trusted to be likeminded, there can be a degree of risk. In a group where being transparent was thought to be safe, and in which I participated years ago, a topic was being discussed where I shared my own personal struggles with a sense of insufficiency (inadequacy) for different situations that occur in ministry. A fellow minister who was present, and for whom I had the highest esteem, looked at me and said: “How disappointing! I thought you had your act together.” This brother in Christ continued to be a good friend throughout his life but his response caught me by surprise and added a safeguard for me that I was hoping could’ve been removed or avoided. It can leave one with a mental barrier in terms of transparency and questions whether or not the other is prepared spiritually and mentally for personal interaction and mutual transparency.

The words of Jesus Christ: “Come! Follow Me! I will make you…” were spoken with authority. Part of their following Jesus Christ and learning from Him are not just instructional. There is an application that each disciple must make in his life. It is not merely group think but part of what is intended in transformational living. This was always present in the words Jesus spoke to larger groups of people during His ministry (John 8:31-32), “If you continue in My word, you are truly My disciples. Then you will know the truth, and the truth will set you free.” These words and actions force one to see that spiritual lives are to be lived intentionally and not accidentally. It requires one to deal with and address loyalties and commitments. The question to be asked individually is: Am I remaining conformed to the world with its values and priorities, or am I being spiritually transformed by the renewal of my mind so that I am enabled to discern the good, perfect and acceptable will of God?

Three passages of Scripture, that should be indelibly traced in our heart, mind and soul, are those that are encouraging and sustaining for one's personal life. They are:

> For Confidence - *Ephesians 3:20, Now to Him who is able to do infinitely more than all we ask or imagine, according to His power that is at work within us...*
>
> For Faith and Prayer - *Isaiah 65:24, It will also come to pass that before they call, I will answer; and while they are still speaking, I will hear.*
>
> For Assurance of God's Faithfulness, *Psalm 37:23-27, The Lord makes firm the steps of the one who delights in him; though he may stumble, he will not fall, for the Lord upholds him with his hand. I was young and now I am old, yet I have never seen the righteous forsaken or their children begging bread.*

For my wife and me, there were several other Scripture passages that influenced us at particular junctures of our lives. As we approached marriage in 1956, we wanted to summarize what our expectations would be for our years together. We were both in immediate agreement that our focus would be the words of Hebrews 12:2 (NASB), "Fixing our eyes on Jesus, the author and perfecter of faith." It was engraved in our hearts and minds. It was also engraved in our wedding rings and on our wedding invitations. For us, this was part of our living the intentional Christian life. It was a viable and visible part of the transformation and transparency process. It focused on the place for the renewing of our minds and will that would enable us to perceive and realize the good, acceptable and perfect will of God for us (Romans 12:2).

In today's religious culture, there seems to be an absence of accepting the deep things of God and His Word. Many are more willing to live a life that is accidental and haphazard than defined, intentional and committed. What can be done in terms of Biblical discipleship so generations to come will have direction and purpose for their lives and culture?

In a Blog, The Outer Monologue by Andy Webb for October 30, 2015 (Used by Permission), he wrote:

> *I was listening to a show on Christian radio yesterday and the host mentioned that what American Christians need and want is deep, compelling, convicting, expository, and doctrinal preaching. She's not the first person I've heard on the radio who has made a statement along those lines, and of course the callers all agree with those sentiments. I, however, am not so sure. I certainly agree that American Christians NEED that kind of preaching, but I'm far less convinced that they WANT that kind of preaching.*

He raises an excellent point when he continues:

> *The churches that are most popular with Christians are the ones where the sermons are light, entertaining, topical, amusing, anecdotal, doctrine-free, and generally about 15 to 25 minutes long. There are a few exceptions, but the rule still applies. Light and fluffy is what draws crowds. So why is there a big difference between what Christians SAY they want to hear, and what they actually choose to listen to on Sunday? I think part of the answer might lie in what one ad man I heard called the "Wonder Bread Rule." He described how when mothers were surveyed in the 1980s about the kind of bread they wanted their family to eat, most said they wanted them to eat natural, whole grain, nourishing wheat breads, with thick chewy crusts. However, when those same moms were surveyed as to their actual buying habits it was found that the majority of them actually bought "Wonder Bread" style breads – soft, bleached white breads, with little or no actual nutritional value. When asked about the*

difference, most explained that Wonder Bread was what their family preferred to eat and that they didn't want to have to deal with the hassle and complaints associated with getting them to eat the things that would actually be good for them.

His concluding thought is poignant and piercing:

Most Christians probably know what kind of 'whole wheat' preaching they need, but they are deathly afraid of the family being bored or irritated or overtaxed by it, and instead choose the Wonder Bread path of least resistance. It may have little or no nutritional value, but its attractive, easy to consume and produces the least complaints.

A question to ponder is whether or not this trend is a new phenomenon. It seems obvious that the Apostle Paul had to cope with a similar mentality. Attention needs to be given to what should be done to reverse this trend toward fluff and to create an appetite for the meat of the Word. We glean some frustration on the part of Paul when he wrote to the Church at Corinth, First Corinthians 3:1-3 (ESV):

Brothers, I could not address you as spiritual, but as worldly, as infants in Christ. I gave you milk, not solid food, for you were not yet ready for solid food. In fact, you are still not ready, for you are still worldly. For since there is jealousy and dissension among you, are you not worldly? Are you not walking in the way of man?

A similar frustration is expressed in Hebrews 5:11-14,

We have much to say about this, but it is hard to explain, because you are dull of hearing. Although by this time you ought to be teachers, you need someone to reteach you the basic principles of God's word. You

> *need milk, not solid food! Everyone who lives on milk is still an infant, inexperienced in the message of righteousness. But solid food is for the mature, who by constant use have trained their sensibilities to distinguish good from evil.*

Is there a solution for the emaciated and weakened visible Church of the twenty-first century? The solution will not be easy. It will take fortitude, determination, added strength and confidence that God's work being done in God's way will bring God's result. It is always all about God and His purpose! The closing words recorded in the Gospel of Matthew 28:18-20 contain the challenge and mandate of Jesus to His disciples regarding the mission and ministry of discipleship: "Jesus came to them and said, All authority in heaven and on earth has been given to me. Therefore, go and make disciples of all nations, baptizing them in the name of the Father and of the Son and of the Holy Spirit, and teaching them to obey everything I have commanded you. And surely, I am with you always, to the very end of the age."

These closing words of Jesus Christ for all generations should be of encouragement as the task of discipleship is undertaken, "And surely I am with you always, to the very end of the age." When we come to obstacles in ministry that appear to be insurmountable, we can lean on the everlasting arms and be confident in His words: "I am with you always, to the very end of the age."

A key to this is that the one espousing discipleship must live a very disciplined life. There is an interesting footnote in the Dictionary.com definition for a disciple. It is one who "believes His doctrine; rests on His sacrifice; imbibes His spirit; and imitates His example" (See: Matthew 10:24, Luke 14:26-27, 33; John 6:69).

I posted some thoughts about this in a Blog on October 27, 2015 titled, Disciplined Discipleship. I began by asking:

> *Have we arrived at a place in life where the culture is allowed to dictate the values and disciplines for entire societies? Who or what is allowed to dictate the terms of behavior and action? Is there any true standard remaining where one can reference the moral, ethical and acceptable behavior that is to be common for the entire human race? When we observe a world that is being marked more and more by upheaval, distrust, and opportunism, it appears that the most assertive and ruthless is dominating a world that has been lackadaisical and indifferent to foundational values and disciplines. It is not just the societal structures that have moved in this direction but the visible Church as well. Once the boundaries are no longer preserved or guarded the greater is the disregard of the warning signs that a slippery slope is imminent and destruction will soon occur. In the secular world, rogue and opportunistic nations are on the move to attain their goal of recognition and domination. When abandonment of values infiltrates the spiritual world, the negative influences and the readiness to accommodate cultural trends begins to emerge. It occurs slowly at first but very soon accelerates until it totally dominates one's life and landscape.*

The Psalmist observed and asked a thought-provoking question in Psalm 11:2-3,

> *The wicked bend their bows; they set their arrows against the strings to shoot from the shadows at the upright in heart. When the foundations are being destroyed, what can the righteous do?*

David not only asked the question, he also offered a response regarding that which will ultimately happen, Psalm 11:5-7,

The Lord examines the righteous, but the wicked, those who love violence, he hates with a passion. On the wicked he will rain fiery coals and burning sulfur; a scorching wind will be their lot. For the Lord is righteous, he loves justice; the upright will see his face.

Between the observation and the ultimate resolution, what are the "righteous" expected to be and do? Should there be a militia formed to combat the evil advances with human weapons and strategies? Should the words of an old Hymn, "Onward Christian Soldiers, marching as to war; With the cross of Jesus going on before…" be interpreted as a physical and militant approach to the issues of the day? The instruction of Paul in Second Corinthians 10:3-5 (NASB) is.

For though we walk in the flesh, we do not war according to the flesh, for the weapons of our warfare are not of the flesh, but divinely powerful for the destruction of fortresses. We are destroying speculations and every lofty thing raised up against the knowledge of God, and we are taking every thought captive to the obedience of Christ.

The force of Scripture is that we are to be marked by an obedience to Ephesians 6:10-13.

Finally, be strong in the Lord and in his mighty power. Put on the full armor of God, so that you can take your stand against the devil's schemes. For our struggle is not against flesh and blood, but against the rulers, against the authorities, against the powers of this dark world and against the spiritual forces of evil in the heavenly realms. Therefore, put on the full armor of God, so that when the day of evil comes, you may be able to stand your ground, and after you have done everything, to stand.

Several years ago, Dr. V. Raymond Edman wrote a book, The Disciplines of Life, in which he stated:

> *Discipleship means 'discipline!' The disciple is that one who has been taught or trained by the Master, who has come with his ignorance, superstition, and sin, to find learning, truth, and forgiveness from the Savior. Without discipline we are not disciples, even though we profess His Name and pass for a follower of the lowly Nazarene. In an undisciplined age when liberty and license have replaced law and loyalty, there is greater need than ever before that we be disciplined to be His disciples... It is His sons whom God disciplines that they might bring honor to His name. He wants to teach and train them, to soften and sweeten them, to strengthen and steady them, that they may show forth the excellencies of Him who told them, Learn of me; for I am meek and lowly in heart: and ye shall find rest unto your souls (Matthew 11:29). Without discipline we are not His sons; but as His own we need the exhortation, 'My son, despise not thou the chastening of the Lord, nor faint when thou art rebuked of him; for whom the Lord loves he chastens, and scourges every son who he receives' (Hebrews 12:5, 6). This discipline at the moment may not seem 'to be joyous, but (rather) grievous: nevertheless, afterward it yields the peaceable fruit of righteousness unto them which are exercised thereby' (Hebrews 12:11).*

Where do we find ourselves today? Are we conformed to the world or transformed by the renewing of our mind? Are we experiencing and seeking after the transformation of body, soul and spirit through the ongoing work of the Holy Spirit in us? Are we disciplined or undisciplined? Are we bent on doing whatever we deem to be right in our own eyes or are we learning obedience to and from our Lord and Master Jesus Christ? Do we adhere to His instruction and guidance or do we stubbornly resist and do our own thing in our own way? Are we more like the straying sheep of Isaiah 53:6 or the responsive sheep of John 10:27 who listen to The Shepherd's voice and eagerly follow Him? The words of Dorothy A. Thrupp penned in 1836 should resonate with us and be the prayer we frequently express (personalize the words by making the plurals, such as "us and we" by expressing them as "me and I"):

Saviour, like a shepherd lead us,
Much we need Thy tender care;
In Thy pleasant pastures feed us,
For our use Thy folds prepare.
Blessed Jesus, blessed Jesus!
Thou hast bought us, Thine we are.
We are Thine, Thou dost befriend us,
Be the guardian of our way;
Keep Thy flock, from sin defend us,
Seek us when we go astray.
Blessed Jesus, blessed Jesus!
Hear, O hear us when we pray.

(Cyber Hymnal – Eminent Domain)

8. My Power Resource

We have not ceased to pray for you and to ask that you may be filled with the knowledge of His will in all spiritual wisdom and understanding, so that you will walk in a manner worthy of the Lord, to please Him in all respects, bearing fruit in every good work and increasing in the knowledge of God; strengthened with all power, according to His glorious might, for the attaining of all steadfastness and patience; joyously giving thanks to the Father, who has qualified us to share in the inheritance of the saints in Light.

Colossians 1:9-12 (NASB)

Following the dynamic preaching of Peter and the ensuing result on the day of Pentecost (Acts 2), the Apostles remained on the cutting edge of what they had sought and attained in the upper room. The power of the Holy Spirit came upon them in dramatic fashion and they were now able to accomplish exploits for the Lord. It must be remembered that these were ordinary men who were being enabled to do extraordinary ministry in the name of the Lord Jesus Christ. They persisted in prayer and remained in the upper room until it was obvious their prayer was answered. At that point they were compelled to go from their secluded place into a hostile world that had recently crucified the Lord Jesus Christ. These men were emboldened and empowered to face the challenges before them. They would take any risk and face any foe for the sake and purpose of the One who had commissioned them. The commissioning moment and promise of Jesus Christ would not be forgotten by them. Matthew 28:16-20 (NASB) records,

> *But the eleven disciples proceeded to Galilee, to the mountain which Jesus had designated. When they saw Him, they worshiped Him; but some were doubtful. And Jesus came up and spoke to them, saying, All authority has been given to Me in heaven and on earth. Go therefore and make disciples of all the nations, baptizing them in the name of the Father and the Son and the Holy Spirit, teaching them to observe all that I commanded you; and lo, I am with you always, even to the end of the age.*

*The Greek word for authority (exousia) conveys the idea of "the power of authority."

The twenty-first century professing Christian and church is marked by hesitancy when it comes to persisting in prayer and too often has its attention diverted to other considerations with a focus upon facilities rather than the commissioning function. Generally, the focus and attention is upon budgetary needs and constraints rather than the ministry of function to seek the lost and needy. It seems as though the Church has gotten its function upside down when it comes to fearless and bold ministry. The apostles were never more concerned about buildings and finances but was always upon the Gospel and the power of God to redeem and transform lives. One day, in retrospect, some churches may find themselves at a place of self-examination where they may muse – "If Only" – we had chosen a different path when we had the opportunity to do so. This is reminiscent of the scenario in Matthew 25:1-13 when Jesus states a parable about the ten virgins and their preparation for the coming of The Bridegroom. The crux of the parable is to be prepared, ready and anticipate the soon coming of The Bridegroom. Five of the virgins took a serious God seriously and had sufficient oil for their lamps and were ready to trim their wicks very quickly. They believed His coming could be imminent. Five thought they would have sufficient time to make preparations and to be ready. Matthew 28:5-6 states, "As the bridegroom was delayed, they all became drowsy and slept. But at midnight there was a cry: Here is the bridegroom! Come out to meet him." The five unprepared asked the five who had made preparation to share their oil with them. They declined to do so. Delayed obedience is always costly! It can also be construed as disobedience.

The unprepared knew the hour was late and time was short for them to locate a merchant who could sell them some oil. By the time they located a merchant, purchased oil for their lamps, trimmed the wicks and returned to the place where the Bridegroom had entered – they were too late. Matthew 25:12-15 (NASB) contains the words of consequence for the unprepared and disobedient,

> *And while they were going away to make the purchase, the bridegroom came, and those who were ready went in with him to the wedding feast; and the door was shut. Later the other virgins also came, saying, Lord, lord, open up for us.*

This scene reminds one of Noah making preparation for the cleansing judgment of God by a flood. When the precise time occurred, Genesis 7:13-16 (NASB) records,

> *On the very same day Noah and Shem and Ham and Japheth, the sons of Noah, and Noah's wife and the three wives of his sons with them, entered the ark, they and every beast after its kind, and all the cattle after their kind, and every creeping thing that creeps on the earth after its kind, and every bird after its kind, all sorts of birds. So they went into the ark to Noah, by twos of all flesh in which was the breath of life. Those that entered, male and female of all flesh, entered as God had commanded him; and the Lord closed it behind him.*

There is an underlying principle that discloses the way in which God works and carries out His will. It is stated in Revelation 3:7 (NLT),

> *This is the message from the one who is holy and true, the one who has the key of David. What he opens, no one can close; and what he closes, no one can open.*

In Noah's day, those who chose to ignore the message of the preacher of righteousness realized there was a point at which the opportunity to hear and heed the warnings from God would terminate. The same is true for the words of Jesus pertaining to the ten virgins. They had all been given the word to the imminent coming of the Bridegroom but only one-half prepared for the any moment appearance. When the announcement is made, five are totally unprepared and must go at a late hour to become prepared. By the time they return, it was too late. Just as the door of the Ark had been closed and sealed by God, even so, after the Bridegroom arrived and entered, The Lord shut and sealed the door. For the five virgins who attempted to become prepared, they had done too little too late.

God can and will select ordinary people to accomplish His objectives that may be seen as extraordinary circumstances or needs. In a devotional from Get More Strength for the Journey by Joseph Stowell, May 22, 2016 entitled: Speak Up! an example is cited from Second Kings 5:3, "If only my master were with the prophet who is in Samaria! For he would heal him of his leprosy." Joseph Stowell wrote:

> *If you're like most people, you think that when God does something important, He uses important people to get it done—people like John Stott, Billy Graham, or Joni Eareckson Tada. The rest of us just fill space until Jesus comes. But that's not true. Most often in Scripture, we see that God uses ordinary folk to get*

things done. Just take a look at the unlikely prophets of the Old Testament and the disciples of the New Testament.

The girl in II Kings 5 was just an ordinary servant. Yet she bravely suggested that Naaman go to the prophet of Israel for healing. What sounds like a simple request was actually a bold suggestion. For Naaman to go to Israel, it would mean turning his back on the local pagan gods, inviting criticism from his countrymen for putting the military might of his nation at risk.

This nameless servant could have paid a steep price for making a suggestion like that, but she knew where the true source of healing was. Because of her deep concern for Naaman's well-being, she courageously put herself at risk to direct him to that source—the one and only living God. Like this young servant girl, let's be willing to be used by God to guide family and friends to the true source of hope and healing.

Very few people think in terms of the imminent or immediate. It is natural to think one has a lot of time to do all that needs to be done. Remember the truth stated above that delayed obedience has consequences because it is actually disobedience to God. Internal change needs to occur in one's soul and spirit. There must be a new or renewed focus on the plans and purposes of God. All of us need to have a greater sense of the urgency in declaring the Gospel to a generation that has ignored the Lord. There is the need to deal in the immediate rather than in the realm of sometime or later on. Charles H. Spurgeon had such a focus when he preached and wrote about, A Free Grace Promise (1888),

Oh, that the unconverted among you may be moved to pray. Before you leave this place, breathe an earnest

> *prayer to God, saying, God be merciful to me a sinner. Lord, I need to be saved. Save me. I call upon thy name. Join with me in prayer at this moment, I entreat you. Join with me while I put words into your mouths, and speak them on your behalf—"Lord, I am guilty. I deserve thy wrath. Lord I cannot save myself. Lord, I would have a new heart and a right spirit, but what can I do? Lord, I can do nothing, come and work in me to will and to do of thy good pleasure. Thou alone hast power, I know, To save a wretch like me; To whom, or whither should I go If I should turn from thee? But I now do from my very soul call upon thy name. Trembling, yet believing, I cast myself wholly upon thee, O Lord. I trust the blood and righteousness of thy dear Son; I trust thy mercy, and thy love, and thy power, as they are revealed in him. I dare to lay hold upon this word of thine, that whosoever shall call on the name of the Lord shall be saved. Lord, save me tonight, for Jesus' sake. Amen.*

The words he spoke and penned are clear, precise and contain the sense of urgency for the immediate. When Peter preached on The Day of Pentecost, Acts 2, he was bold, clear, and precise to the point of bluntness. A characteristic of his preaching is that it was powerful and called for an immediate response. The result of his directness is recorded in Acts 2:37-41,

> *Now when they heard this, they were pierced to the heart, and said to Peter and the rest of the apostles, Brethren, what shall we do? Peter said to them, Repent, and each of you be baptized in the name of Jesus Christ for the forgiveness of your sins; and you will receive the gift of the Holy Spirit. For the promise is for you and your children and for all who are far off, as many as the Lord our God will call to Himself. And*

with many other words he solemnly testified and kept on exhorting them, saying, Be saved from this perverse generation! So then, those who had received his word were baptized; and that day there were added about three thousand souls.

There would be other instances when the presence of the power of God was evidenced. When they were united together in ministry and prayer, Acts 4:31-32 records,

And when they had prayed, the place where they had gathered together was shaken, and they were all filled with the Holy Spirit and began to speak the word of God with boldness. And the congregation of those who believed were of one heart and soul.

Whenever there was praise and prayer on the part of the people, there was also the presence and the power of Holy Spirit. Most of the Book of Acts records that reality. Do you believe there is a place for prayer and praise in the Church today? Do you believe it would also invite the presence and the power of God to be in the midst of His people? Your answer should be, "Yes!"

Another example of the unity of God's people in praise and prayer is given in Acts 12. The situation is one of great concern because Peter's life and freedom are the issue. Acts 12:1-2,

Now about that time Herod the king laid hands on some who belonged to the church in order to mistreat them. And he had James the brother of John put to death with a sword.

A problem with a despot like Herod is that when the populace seems to respond positively to his antagonistic actions it motivates him to go further and to wreak as much havoc as possible. Acts 12:3-4,

> *When he (Herod) saw that it pleased the Jews, he proceeded to arrest Peter also. Now it was during the days of Unleavened Bread. When he had seized him, he put him in prison, delivering him to four squads of soldiers to guard him, intending after the Passover to bring him out before the people.*

Herod's thought was to have a response from the people similar to when Jesus was brought before the crowds. Perhaps the people will cry out to crucify Peter just as they had cried out against Jesus. Herod failed to consider and recognize how prayer and praise will bring a result of God's presence and power in the immediate situation. It is not surprising to read what a committed people did in Acts 12:5, "So Peter was kept in the prison, but prayer for him was being made fervently by the church to God." The key is "fervent prayer" was being offered by a united group of God's people. They were intense as they came before the Lord and were confident that God would respond positively. The remainder of the chapter indicates that an Angel of the Lord appeared; the chains of Peter fell off; he followed the Angel and the prison doors opened and he was freed by the presence and power of the Lord.

As the people fervently prayed, did they expect the Lord's intervention, opening prison doors and releasing Peter? Did they anticipate Peter knocking at their gate so he could join their prayer gathering and praise the Lord for his release? Acts 12:16 is so descriptive of the way too many people pray. People say the appropriate words but they do not expect the ensuing result. The scene is so real. The people keep praying! Peter keeps knocking at the door to gain admission! The people do not believe he could've been miraculously released. "But Peter continued knocking; and when they had opened the door, they saw him and were amazed." Is this the way we tend to pray? We pray with intensity and urgency but do we look with anticipation and expectancy for God's answer? Do we leave his answer knocking at the gate while we keep on praying for that answer? The lesson they would learn from the Lord was the reality of unchained expectancy as He demonstrated that He is the power, the omnipotent (all-powerful) resource for all of His people.

One of the unique features of the book of Acts is its frequent reference to prayer. In reading through the various chapters, the occurrence of "and when they had prayed" (or some variation of that activity) appears often. It is attached to the ministry resulting in both evangelism and church growth. When we entertain these designs and ministry purpose for Christ and His Church, whatever is contemplated or planned should be first saturated with fervent and frequent prayer. When this is the commitment, there can be an expectation for God's intervention, blessing and powerful working beyond any human contemplation.

There are anchor and summary verses throughout the book of Acts. The initial effort of the Apostles and believers after the ascension of Jesus Christ, even though there was political action, persecution and personal hardship as opponents sought to eliminate the name of Jesus from the ministry cause, was:

> *The word of God kept on spreading; and the number of the disciples continued to increase greatly..."* (Acts 6:7 - NASB).

The opposition and persecution was intense. Despite the best efforts of the negative influences, imprisonment of believers, persecution and the martyrdom of a dynamic and faithful servant of the Lord, Stephen, there was a positive result and summary recorded in Acts 9:31 (NASB),

> *So the church throughout all Judea and Galilee and Samaria enjoyed peace, being built up; and going on in the fear of the Lord and in the comfort of the Holy Spirit, it continued to increase.*

These are the words following the best efforts of Saul of Tarsus as he represented the political and religious leaders of his day. With letters of persecution, he sought to wreak havoc and destroy anyone who was declaring Jesus Christ and His Gospel. Far removed from his personal ambitions was the thought that he would become a follower of the very one he was trying to extinguish from public discourse. The martyrdom of Stephen and others did not prevent the impact of the Gospel on the lives of people.

In a summary of the historical impact of the Church it is recorded as common knowledge that Tertullian (AD 197) declared, "The blood of martyrs is the seed of the Christian." This phrase has been duplicated with various emphases, the most common of which is: "The blood of the martyrs is the seed of the Church." It also seems obvious that this was gleaned from the way God was working through His faithful servants in The Book of Acts.

King Herod was relentless in his effort to silence all Christians and their message. Acts 12 records his actions toward James, whom he had killed, and Peter, who was imprisoned until the mob of opposition could be organized to demand his death as well. The many despots referenced through Holy Scripture refused to learn the basic lesson that God has absolute power and will accomplish His absolute will. Despite Herod's threats, imprisonments, murder and plans to continue on this pathway, another anchor verse avers, "But the word of the Lord continued to grow and to be multiplied (Acts 12:24 - NASB). Throughout Acts 12, God's people fearlessly gathered and fervently prayed for God's intervention. What is the potential and possibility for The Twenty-First Century Church if it followed the example of the first century Church? Do you believe God still hears the urgent plea and fervent prayer of His people today?

Following the events as they unfolded in Acts 12, a transition takes place in The Book of Acts when Saul of Tarsus, the persecutor, becomes a convert to the Christianity he was trying to eliminate. He will be transformed as he becomes the Apostle Paul, the proclaimer. One of the anchor verses that summarizes the ongoing work and witness of the Church of Jesus Christ is Acts 16:5 (NASB), "So the churches were being strengthened in the faith and were increasing in number daily." The presence of prayer and a persistent praying people continued. There was recognition that the power of God was best accessed by prayer and the presence of God in their midst.

Charles Haddon Spurgeon preached many sermons on the subject of prayer. One of them was based upon Psalm 119:37 (KJV), "Turn away mine eyes from beholding vanity; and quicken thou me in Thy way." Part of that sermon included the following:

> *I think you will find the prayer for quickening repeated nine times in this Psalm. The form of it differs, but it is always the same vehement cry, "Quicken me, O Lord." In addition to this, you will hear David twice acknowledge that God had quickened him, saying on one occasion, "Your Word has quickened me," and in another place, "Your Precepts have quickened me"; so that 11 times in one Psalm David turns his contemplations to the subject of quickening, and this shows us the very great importance which he attached to it. Remember well that this Psalm is dedicated to the praise of the Word of God. Throughout its entire length it sounds forth the honor of God's statutes, and in some way or other the Word of the Lord is mentioned in every one of its 176 verses. The Psalm is a star of the first magnitude, and all its beams direct us to the Divine Statutes; it is clear from this that there must be an intimate connection between quickening*

> *and the Word of God; indeed, it is so, for when we are much acquainted with the Word of God, we also discover more of our own deadness and lack of spiritual life!*

The text, Psalm 119:37, is rendered with slight difference in modern translations. The NLT states it: "Turn my eyes from worthless things and give me life through your word." The ESV renders it: "Turn my eyes from looking at worthless things; and give me life in your ways." The NIV records it as: "Turn my eyes away from worthless things; preserve my life according to your word." Regardless of the translation selected, the truth is twofold, First, the place for fervent prayer so that one may be transitioned from a state of death to newness of life in Christ. Second, the Word of God is always the reference point in terms of spiritual life. Hebrews 4:12-13 (ESV) instructs us in terms of our need for knowing and doing the Word of God. The words recorded are:

> *For the word of God is living and active, sharper than any two-edged sword, piercing to the division of soul and of spirit, of joints and of marrow, and discerning the thoughts and intentions of the heart. And no creature is hidden from his sight, but all are naked and exposed to the eyes of him to whom we must give account.*

How consistent is your exposure to The Living and Active Word of God? How essential do you believe this exposure must be connected to your commitment to fervent prayer? Are these things part of the fabric of your spiritual life? Do you know the freedom that ensues from being unchained from the things that would bind and hinder you from the fullness of the life in Christ that is to be full and complete?

There are two additional anchor verses in The Book of Acts that summarize the ministry motivated by fervent prayer and firm commitment to the Gospel and all Scripture. The anchor verses seem to summarize certain periods of time from the Ascension of Jesus Christ up to A.D. 65 when Nero unleashed his opposition to the Christian sect. Despite the opposition along the way, Acts 19:20 (NASB) interjects a summary of the ongoing ministry expressing: "The Word of God grew mightily and prevailed."

The final anchor point appears to be very abrupt. It is thought that the lives of those who were serving the Lord and writing abruptly lost their lives during Nero's persecution. Luke's words in Acts 28:30-31 (NASB) are a record of Paul's house arrest and the manner of his ministry, "And he stayed two full years in his own rented quarters and was welcoming all who came to him, preaching the kingdom of God and teaching concerning the Lord Jesus Christ with all openness, unhindered."

The overall point is that any work of God must include reliance upon the fervent prayer of God's servants and people. It is a vital part of advancing the cause of Jesus Christ. The believers and the Church also need to be firmly committed to God's Word in its entirety. Many times the Church resorts to methods that are supposed to result in church growth. There are seminars and courses designed to achieve reasonable goals in terms of growth. While there is nothing wrong with being motivated and better equipped to doing a task with the goal of being successful, there should never be the diminishing of the Biblical and spiritual approach to doing God's work in God's way so that it will accomplish God's will and God's purpose. Nowhere in Scripture is the Church called to gimmickry.

The Church's mandate is to preach the Gospel; to make disciples of all people regardless of ethnicity or nation of origin; and to incorporate them into the bride of Christ, His

Church. Wherever people are located, there is opportunity for the mandate of Jesus Christ to be effectively implemented.

May God richly bless you as you seek Him on His terms! Be bold and courageous as you reach out to the multitudes of souls who are in bondage and enslaved to sin. They need exposure to the reality of Jesus Christ living in a person. This means the messenger must have that presence of the Lord exuding from his/her life. The shackled souls need to hear the liberating message of the Gospel by which they can enter into unchained expectancy because Jesus Christ has unshackled them and set them free indeed.

9. Intentional Living

I remind you to fan into flame the gift of God, which is in you through the laying on of my hands, for God gave us a spirit not of fear but of power and love and self-control (a sound mind). Therefore, do not be ashamed of the testimony about our Lord, nor of me his prisoner, but share in suffering for the gospel by the power of God, who saved us and called us to a holy calling, not because of our works but because of his own purpose and grace, which he gave us in Christ Jesus before the ages began.

II Timothy 1:6-9 (ESV)

As we observe our world and culture, there is cause for concern. As we observe the twenty-first century Church and the professing Christians attending it, there is occasion for further concern. Are we able to observe the words of Paul in Second Timothy 1:7 activated in either the twenty-first century Church or the lives of professing Christians, "God gave us a spirit not of fear but of power and love and self-control (a sound mind)"? How well are these words implemented in our lives today? We find ourselves paralyzed by some undetermined force. Fear overwhelms us; timidity causes us to withdraw; and love seems to be increasingly remote. Our thought processes and rationale seem to be neutralized. The whole idea of self-control and a sound mind seem to be distant and remote. If this is valid within the twenty-first century culture, world and Church, is there a way to become unshackled and set free from the trends and cultural demands? Has an irreligious sentiment been allowed to alter the moral standards and core values of our culture and world?

A news item contained a passing observation about the status of religion in France: "71% of the French say religion is unimportant to them and fewer than 4.5% attend weekly church services" (National Review, June 26, 2016). A generalized observation about religion and church attendance in the United States, while not being as dismal as that of France, is that they are trending in the same direction. A question that should be considered is whether or not one's religious commitment and church attendance in the United States of America is more intentional than accidental.

What is the basis for moral values and ethical choices in the culture and church today? How does a culture or society become what it is? Are these, and other areas of life, a result of intentional choices or accidental occurrences? These and other thoughts began to resonate as I read the review of John Maxwell's book entitled: "Intentional Living: Choosing A Life That Matters." His own shared testimony states:

> *Living intentionally will motivate you to start asking questions and begin prioritizing whatever is important to you. Can I make a difference? Whom should I help? How can I help them? How can I add value to them?*

I'm indebted to a friend who directed my attention to the Calvinist Methodist movement. In 1729, while John Wesley was a student at Oxford, he started a club with his brother Charles. It was soon mockingly dubbed "The Holy Club" by some of his fellow collegians. Despite the mockery of some, the club members (never more than twenty-five members) rigorously self-examined themselves everyday by asking twenty-two questions. Some of them were:

> *Am I consciously or unconsciously creating the impression that I am better than I really am? In other words, am I a hypocrite?*
>
> *Am I honest in all my acts and words, or do I exaggerate?*
>
> *Do I confidentially pass on to others what has been said to me in confidence?*

Can I be trusted?
Did the Bible live in me today?
Do I give the Bible time to speak to me every day?
Am I enjoying prayer?
When did I last speak to someone else of my faith?
Do I disobey God in anything?
Is there anyone whom I fear, dislike, disown, criticize, hold a resentment toward or disregard? If so, what am I doing about it?
Do I grumble or complain constantly?
Is Christ real to me?

A Biblical basis for this accountability group was Hebrews 3:12-13 (NKJV),

> *Beware, brethren, lest there be in any of you an evil heart of unbelief in departing from the living God; but exhort (encourage) one another daily, while it is called "Today," lest any of you be hardened through the deceitfulness of sin.*

We should remind ourselves that each of us represents a person who possesses tremendous potential. If each of us lived up to that possibility and potential, it would revolutionize not only our personal lives but other lives with whom we have any meaningful and purposeful relationship. The key to realizing this significance and potential is to reply as the disciples did when they heard these words of Jesus Christ: "Come! Follow Me! I will make you…" The words of Jesus were clear, precise and spoken with authority. The response of those who were being called as disciples was immediate: "At once they left their nets and followed Him" (Matthew 4:20). Inherent in their following Jesus Christ and learning from Him are the words Jesus spoke to larger groups of people during His ministry (John 8:31-32), "If you continue in My word, you are truly My disciples. Then you will know the truth, and the truth will set you free." These words and actions force one to see that spiritual lives are to be lived intentionally and not accidentally.

The interviewer and reviewer of John Maxwell's book shares his personal reflections when reviewing the thoughts on intentional living.

> *In Intentional Living, Maxwell discusses his struggles with personal flaws such as selfishness and opens up about the role his faith plays in his life of significance. My life is flawed, yet I believe I need to share it with you in a way I never have before because I don't know of any better way to teach you how to embark upon intentional living, Maxwell declares early on in the book. I believe that if you know my story and how it unfolded, it will help you to write your own story of significance. It will empower you to lead yourself to a life that matters.*

There can be always be a degree of risk when pursuing intentional living and transparent ministry. Anytime there is transparency, there is a possibility of risk. Why? There can be a breach in confidentiality and data shared with a wider circle of people than one expected or wanted. It is similar to the operating principles used by AA (Alcoholics Anonymous) or NA (Narcotics Anonymous). Transparency and confidentiality are connected to each other. Any breach at this point would violate the trust factor that is inherent with transparency and confidentiality. AA and NA are support groups founded upon the need for transparency and the willingness to seek release from whatever addiction that has infiltrated and taken over one's life. There is a requirement that is obvious, namely, one must walk the walk about which he/she is talking. It is not a place for hypocrisy or time to act erudite, superior or even acting in a condescending manner. Confidentially is an integral part of support groups.

Another factor is that too often some people with whom we have contact are prone to take others for granted or in a dismissive way. How we interpret and categorize one another should be of great concern. The words of Romans 15:7 should be indelibly written in in our hearts and minds: "Accept one another, just as Jesus Christ also accepted us to the glory of God."

A question one would do well to ask is: Whatever happened to an emphasis upon intentional Christian living within the charter and purpose of the Church as well as in the mission statement that is used to determine both focus and investment of time, talent and outreach? When you look around the local Church and those in attendance at a worship service, do you ever wonder why they have come? Are they in attendance due to a firm conviction that it is a matter of obedience to God's Word in Hebrews 10:24-25, or some other reason? The Scripture states:

> *And let us consider how to stir up one another to love and good works, not neglecting to meet together, as is the habit of some, but encouraging one another, and all the more as you see the Day drawing near.*

Several years ago, Dr. A.W. Tozer preached a sermon, Fencing with Masters. There is no indication of his personal observations that led him to make the following statement and while it appears to be a generalization, it is very close to hitting the nail on the head. He is reported to have said:

> *For the time will come when they will not endure sound doctrine, but according to their own desires, because they have itching ears, they will heap up for themselves teachers; and they will turn their ears away from the truth and be turned aside to fables (Second Timothy 4:3-4). Everyone who has come to the years of responsibility seems to have gone on the defensive. Even some of you who have known me for years are*

> *surely on the defensive--you have your guard up all the time! I know that you are not afraid of me, but you are afraid, nevertheless, of what I am going to say. Probably every faithful preacher today is fencing with masters as he faces his congregation. The guard is always up. The quick parry is always ready. It is very hard for me to accept the fact that it is now very rare for anyone to come into the house of God with guard completely down, head bowed and with the silent confession: Dear Lord, I am ready and willing to hear what You will speak to my heart today! We have become so learned and so worldly and so sophisticated and so blasé and so bored and so religiously tired that the clouds of glory seem to have gone from us.*

He then offered a corporate prayer:

> *Lord, quiet my own heart before You and give me that humble spirit of listening. Whenever I come before You (including this morning!), may it be with my guard completely down, head bowed, ready and willing to hear what You will speak to my heart today. Amen.*

Obviously, he was addressing the need for intentional commitment to worship rather than accidental convenience of an appearance to gain acceptance of the church people or one's family. If only those who gather had a mindset for unchained expectancy and a fuller measure of being free indeed. If only the purpose was to seek the Lord with all of one's heart, soul, strength and mind. If only there was the burning within and the breakthrough comparable to when Jacob wrestled with God and desperately declared, "I will not let you go unless you bless me."

The words to an old Hymn of consecration, author unknown, that apply to intentional live are expressed in the fifth stanza:

My heart, my soul, I have resigned
Drink offering for Your joy.
Imagination never could find
Or want greater employ!
I will not let Thee go my Lord,
I will not let Thee go!
Confession glad on Thee outpoured,
Thine own dear heart to know.

One's consecration must be intentional and not accidental. If it borders on the accidental, it can too easily become a fabrication for what it means to be holy as the Lord is holy. As it is, there are far too many clinging to a counterfeit religion. It allows for a view that God is a God of love and not judgment; that heaven is the place where church people will go; any discussion of hell causes some to cringe and disagree; and where walking by the enablement of the Holy Spirit is foreign to one's professed Christianity.

There must be a breakthrough into unchained expectancy and the full realization of being free indeed in Jesus Christ. One must reexamine his or her commitment and ask: Is it intentional or accidental? May this result represent who you are. May it be descriptive of your life and Biblical Christian walk.

Out of my bondage, sorrow, and night,
Jesus, I come! Jesus, I come!
Into Thy freedom, gladness, and light,
Jesus, I come to Thee!

Out of my shameful failure and loss,
Jesus, I come! Jesus, I come!
Into the glorious gain of Thy cross,
Jesus, I come to Thee!

10. Free Indeed

So Jesus said to the Jews who had believed him: If you abide in my word, you are truly my disciples, and you will know the truth, and the truth will set you free. They answered him, We are offspring of Abraham and have never been enslaved to anyone. How is it that you say, You will become free? Jesus answered them, Truly, truly, I say to you, everyone who practices sin is a slave to sin. The slave does not remain in the house forever; the son remains forever. So if the Son sets you free, you will be free indeed...

John 8:31-38, 43-45 (ESV)

The words of Jesus Christ recorded in John 8:36 should resonate with every Biblical Christian, "If the Son sets you free, you will be free indeed." What is it to be "free indeed"? What is the freedom Jesus offers and promises? Galatians 5:1 (NASB) gives a clear response: "It was for freedom that Christ set us free; therefore keep standing firm and do not be subject again to a yoke of slavery." The basic idea of true freedom is the sense and state of being free, with liberty rather than being in confinement or under physical restraint. It includes and concludes that one is free from external control or interference. It extends to one the reality of personal liberty as opposed to bondage or slavery. A part of the heritage for citizens of the United States of America are contained in the words of the Pledge of Allegiance to the flag of the USA. Part of the pledge states we are: "One nation under God, indivisible, with liberty and justice for all.". In the Declaration of Independence are similar words: "We hold these truths to be self-evident, that all men are created equal, that they are endowed by their Creator with life, liberty and the pursuit of happiness."

Within the secular world, liberty and justice can become theory rather than fact. There can be an imbalance in these important areas where income status or ethnic backgrounds are the determining factors of one's experience and appreciation of "liberty and justice for all." One can only wonder if the diminishing of a core value, "one nation under God" is the cause and effect of the cultural abasement that is negating "liberty and justice for all."

By contrast, in the spiritual world, "liberty and justice for all" is a fact rather than fiction. It is because liberty and justice have been secured in and through the redemptive work of Jesus Christ. This truth is declared and defined in passages, such as: Romans 3:24, "We are justified by his grace as a gift, through the redemption that is in Christ Jesus." Also in Ephesians 1:8, "In him (Jesus Christ), we have redemption through his blood, the forgiveness of our trespasses, according to the riches of his grace." Inasmuch as there is a considerable difference between the values of the secular versus the spiritual, we do well to review some of God's provision for all who have turned to Jesus Christ for redemption, renewal and restoration.

The Biblical foundational truth is established, and made available to all of the people of God. This is based upon the statement in Romans 8:21, "The creation itself will be set free from its bondage to corruption and obtain the freedom of the glory of the children of God." From the beginning of time, there has been an evident conflict between the foundations of righteousness and the forces of evil. The effort of the force of evil is to distract and deceive the people of God. In the Garden of Eden, it was the suggestion that God did not mean what he said about partaking of forbidden fruit.

As the Church was being established in the first century, the distraction and deception was to return to circumcision as a requirement for God's people. The Apostle Paul summarizes the devious attempt when he wrote, Galatians 2:4, "Yet because of false brothers secretly brought in who slipped in to spy out our freedom that we have in Christ Jesus, so that they might bring us into slavery…" The design and effort is to distract and deceive the people of God. Such forces are relentless in that effort to undermine the Christian beliefs that are being embraced. Peter makes mention of this, Second Peter 2:19, "They promise them freedom, but they themselves are slaves of corruption. For whatever overcomes a person, to that he is enslaved." Because of this determination to distract and deceive the people of God, numerous warnings were issued by the Apostle Paul. He did it in a context of the persistent and ongoing need to suppress the desires of the flesh and mind because they are contrary to the fruit of the Holy Spirit that is supposed to be manifested in the life of each follower of Jesus Christ. A type of such warning is Galatians 5:13, "For you were called to freedom, brothers. Only do not use your freedom as an opportunity for the flesh, but through love serve one another." It follows through on the emphasis of the Gospel truth that when Jesus Christ sets us free, we will be free indeed (John 8:36).

The message of Jesus Christ to all people groups with whom he was engaged served as a reminder of the clarity of His message. In contrast to the freedom He offers is the bondage and enslavement of those who yield to the desires of the flesh and mind as they continue to practice sin. Jesus stated that such a one is actually a slave to sin. The question can be posed and asked repeatedly, how can that be? What defines one who has willingly rejected freedom in Christ and chosen to be a slave to sin? Anticipating that question, Jesus amplifies His response: (John 8:42-44),

> *You are of your father the devil, and your will is to do your father's desires. He was a murderer from the beginning, and does not stand in the truth, because*

there is no truth in him. When he lies, he speaks out of his own character, for he is a liar and the father of lies. But because I tell the truth, you do not believe me.

There are certain truths about the enemy of one's soul that should be known. We have all heard the phrase (and possibly used it), at one time or another, "The devil made me do it!" Some of the things we should know about the devil, his methods, subtlety, schemes are shared in Second Corinthians 2:5-11,

Now if anyone has caused pain, he has caused it not to me, but in some measure—not to put it too severely—to all of you. For such a one, this punishment by the majority is enough, so you should rather turn to forgive and comfort him, or he may be overwhelmed by excessive sorrow. So I beg you to reaffirm your love for him. For this is why I wrote, that I might test you and know whether you are obedient in everything. Anyone whom you forgive, I also forgive. Indeed, what I have forgiven, if I have forgiven anything, has been for your sake in the presence of Christ, so that we would not be outwitted by Satan; for we are not ignorant of his designs (schemes).

There is a stark difference between the purposes of Jesus Christ and the enemy of your soul. One of the truths we learn about Jesus Christ is His eternal purpose (Luke 19:10), "For the Son of Man came to seek and to save the lost." One of the truths we learn about the purpose of our enemy is his desire to destroy God's people. This was explained succinctly to believers who were being persecuted and scattered in the first century (First Peter 5:8-9, NLT),

Stay alert! Watch out for your great enemy, the devil. He prowls around like a roaring lion, looking for someone to devour. Stand firm against him and be

strong in your faith. Remember that your Christian brothers and sisters all over the world are going through the same kind of suffering you are.

The goal of your enemy is singular – to devour and destroy! Despite the challenge, the twofold admonition is: (1) Stand firm against him, and (2) Be strong in your faith. If you do so, regardless of the persecution and its severity, you will be able to be secure in the freedom by which Christ has set you free.

Your enemy will do whatever is necessary to get you to deviate from the foundational principles of your faith. One verse that should be remembered and applied when these deviations present themselves is Galatians 5:1, "It was for freedom Christ has set us free; stand firm therefore, and do not submit to a yoke of bondage." We will use this verse often to respond to the various and sundry deviations that try to turn us from the pathway of following Jesus Christ alone. Some of the means the enemy employs include:

DISTRACTION: *From the will and purpose of God for your life. Galatians 5:1, It was for freedom Christ has set us free; stand firm therefore, and do not submit to a yoke of Distraction.*

DISCOURAGEMENT: *Getting you to focus on your circumstances rather than on the one who will deliver you. Galatians 5:1, It was for freedom Christ has set us free; stand firm therefore, and do not submit to a yoke of Discouragement.*

DISAPPOINTMENT: *Your greatest hopes seem to have failed and frustration has replaced desire to keep on keeping on. Galatians 5:1, It was for freedom Christ has set us free; stand firm, and do not submit to a yoke of Disappointment.*

DISTRESS: *Becoming overwhelmed mentally and physically by unfolding events that you neither expected or desired. Many times, it results from unintended consequences due to personal choices. Galatians 5:1, It was for freedom Christ has set us free; stand firm therefore, and do not submit to a yoke of distress.*

How does one get into these various situations of distress and anxiety? Jesus explained it with the use of the parable of the sower and the seed, Matthew 13:18-23. Jesus stated:

> *Listen then to what the parable of the sower means: When anyone hears the message about the kingdom and does not understand it, the evil one comes and snatches away what was sown in their heart. This is the seed sown along the path. The seed falling on rocky ground refers to someone who hears the word and at once receives it with joy. But since they have no root, they last only a short time. When trouble or persecution comes because of the word, they quickly fall away. The seed falling among the thorns refers to someone who hears the word, but the worries of this life and the deceitfulness of wealth choke the word, making it unfruitful. But the seed falling on good soil refers to someone who hears the word and understands it. This is the one who produces a crop, yielding a hundred, sixty or thirty times what was sown.*

Perhaps one of the greatest contributors to distress and anxiety is in the category of the worries of this life. What are some of the worries of this life that cause distraction and deviation? One is divorce. There is an inner sense that the love once known has waned and the relationship has diminished. The attraction and desire for oneness is no longer present. It has been replaced by hostility which has allowed a wedge to enter the relationship. It will soon bring about cleavage between a man and a woman. It is at this point where the constant desire is to be away from one another. People arrive at this point because they have forgotten or neglected how God wants His people to view and sanctify marriage.

Many have never known God's expression about divorce that is recorded in Malachi 2:16,

> *For I hate divorce, says The Lord, the God of Israel, and him who covers his garment with wrong, says The Lord of Hosts. So take heed to your spirit, that you do not deal treacherously.*

The heart cry of God is for faithfulness and fidelity in marriage that is based upon and maintained by Agape (intense love expressed by God toward His sinning world to whom He sent His Only Son to be the once-for-all sacrifice for their sins). When marriage counselling is necessary or sought, there is one undergirding principle that is absolute. A husband is to love his wife in the same way God so loved us that He gave His only son to be the sacrifice for one's sins. When there is rabid hostility, coupled with expressed hatred and detesting of a spouse, there are three Biblical love possibilities for the offended or offending person.

> The first possibility *that the Scripture is clear about is the husband wife relationship. Colossians 3:19, "Husbands, love (agape) your wives, and do not be harsh with them." This truth is repeated in Ephesians 5:25, "Husbands, love your wives, just as Christ loved the church and gave Himself up for her." The emphasis that should be noted is that the love a man has for his wife is to be comparable to the love Jesus Christ had for His Bride – the Church. If the man responds that love for his spouse is beyond a possibility because of how much he detests her, there is another love level which the man must consider.*

The second proposed possibility *is the directive for one to love your neighbor. One place where this is expressed is Galatians 5:14, "The entire Law is fulfilled in a single decree: Love (agape) your neighbor as yourself." The application is that one's spouse is the nearest neighbor one has and the directive clearly states that one must love his nearest neighbor. In this scenario, one's wife is the nearest neighbor a man can have! If the man continues to impatiently affirm that he wants nothing to do with his wife any longer because he detests her, there is one more possibility that must be considered.*

The third proposed possibility *is that one is directed to love (agape) your enemy. Jesus Christ issued this directive in Matthew 5:44 where He said: "I tell you, love your enemies and pray for those who persecute you." If the husband continues to be adamant in his expressed hostility, hatred and disdain for his wife, he still must reach a determination regarding at what level he will manifest (agape) love.*

A choice has to be made. There are only three appropriate possibilities. The man must choose which possibility he will embrace and implement. Will he choose to return to having (agape) love for his wife? If not, will he respond affirmatively and choose to have (agape) love for his wife as his nearest neighbor? Or, will he remain in his hostility, hatred and disdain but grudgingly give heed to the directive of Jesus Christ and (agape) love her even as an enemy? The summary remains the same for us who follow Jesus Christ.

DIVORCE: Galatians 5:1, *It was for freedom Christ has set us free; stand firm therefore, and do not submit to a yoke of divorce.*

DEPRESSION: *Body, soul and spirit has begun to suffer from and the absence of a harmonious and homogeneous foundation. It is replaced by that which is discordant. Sometimes, drugs, alcoholic beverages and other mood modifiers become a coping mechanism. Too often, mood modifiers are used as a way of escaping from the pressures and demands of life.*

In regard to depression, a friend (H.S.) shared her personal testimony and graciously granted me permission to use it. It illustrates depression as one of the enemy's lines of attack. She wrote and shared:

I was diagnosed with post-partum depression and lost interest in things I once enjoyed – I didn't want to talk to anyone or really even associate with the world. It was as if a dark cloud had surrounded me.

There didn't seem to be a light at the end of the tunnel. When I became pregnant with my 4th child, I was already struggling with post-partum depression from the birth of my 3rd child.

A doctor prescribed some anti-depressants but then I began suffering from post-partum psychosis and began worrying my husband and everyone else around me.

I was admitted into a mental hospital for a week and was evaluated by doctors. At that time, I was six months pregnant. It was one of the scariest things I have ever been through.

Desperately, I wanted to be home with my husband and kids, but I had to get well first.

I came home after a week, but really wasn't emotionally or mentally ready. Nothing had been changed, as far as the hopelessness I felt.

I was still in the same mindset. I stayed on the anti-depressants until the baby (Sarah) was born.

Sadly, I didn't really have any kind of emotional attachment when I held her. It didn't faze me at all. Then, I decided to stop taking my medicine and that's when things started to go downhill.

I was back to the mental hospital when the baby (Sarah) was just 6 weeks old.

I was so worried that I would never go back home again. That is how it felt in my mind at the time - that this was the last time I would ever see my family again. It was so hopeless I didn't know where to turn, or how to go on living life that way.

I got down on my knees while in the hospital and I prayed that God would heal me of my depression; that He'd give me strength to be the mom and the wife my kids and husband needed me to be. When I came home from the hospital my life would be changed forever.

I know that it's only with God's amazing redemption and grace, that I'm alive and well today! So now I am able to reach out and help others who are struggling with depression and let them know there is a light at the end of the tunnel. That bright and burning light is Jesus Christ!

Despite this progress, H.S. still has moments of relapse and needs someone who is sensitive to her struggle with depression and truly cares about her, to gently and lovingly nudge her back toward Jesus and His readiness to keep her free indeed.

A contemporary alternate version of Amazing Grace expresses the following to every troubled and burdened soul,

The Lord has promised good to me
His word my hope secures

He will my shield and portion be
As long as life endures.

My chains are gone - I've been set free
My God, my Savior has ransomed me
And like a flood His mercy rains
Unending love, Amazing grace.

In 1738 – Charles Wesley Wrote: And Can It Be?

Long my imprisoned spirit lay,
Fast bound in sin and nature's night...
My chains fell off, my heart was free,
I rose, went forth, and followed Thee.

The enemy of one's soul is skilled at masquerading his true identity. Paul wrote about this tactic in Second Corinthians 11:14-15 (ESV), "For even Satan disguises himself as an angel of light." So it is no surprise if his servants, also, disguise themselves as servants of righteousness. Their end will correspond to their deeds." The word translated "disguise" can also be rendered as pretense or masquerade.

We should also know the enemy's strategy. Paul wrote about it in Second Thessalonians 2:9-12,

> *The coming of the lawless one is by the activity of Satan with all power and false signs and wonders, and with all wicked deception for those who are perishing, because they refused to love the truth and so be saved. Therefore, God sends them a strong delusion, so that they may believe what is false, in order that all may be condemned who did not believe the truth but had pleasure in unrighteousness.*

A colleague in ministry (J.F.) shared a thought on Facebook about a Sunday experience in the Church where he serves as Pastor. He wrote:

> *In ministering today, I was reminded of...the devastation of addiction, the pain of divorce, and the sting of death. Thanks be to God for Revelation 21:5 which states, He who was seated on the throne said, I am making everything new! Then he said, Write this down, for these words are trust-worthy and true." For those of you who are struggling this day, be reminded of the great work that God is doing through His Son Jesus. He might not work at the pace we desire, but He cares for His people and He surely is at work!*

How long will this spiritual warfare last? The precise answer is until Jesus Christ returns or by one's physical death. At that point, hope will be fully realized; faith will become sight; and all of God's redeemed ones will be with Him throughout eternity. While awaiting that moment of being in His eternal presence, one must persevere and endure. Paul shared his focus, Philippians 1:20-21,

> *I eagerly expect and hope that I will in no way be ashamed, but will have complete boldness, so that now as always Christ will be exalted in my body, whether by life or by death. For to me, to live is Christ, and to die is gain.*

Paul also avowed in Acts 20:20-24,

> *I did not shrink from declaring to you anything that was profitable and teaching you in public and from house to house, testifying both to Jews and to Greeks of repentance toward God and of faith in our Lord Jesus Christ. And now, behold, I am going to Jerusalem, constrained by the Spirit, not knowing what will happen to me there, except that the Holy Spirit*

testifies to me in every city that imprisonment and afflictions await me. But I do not account my life of any value nor as precious to myself, if only I may finish my course and the ministry that I received from the Lord Jesus, to testify to the gospel of the grace of God.

While we tarry in life and upon this earth, we should constantly remind ourselves and always be grateful for our Lord's provision for us, Galatians 5:1, "It was for freedom Christ has set us free; stand firm therefore, and do not submit to a yoke of slavery/bondage." We are called and designed to be those who enter into unchained expectancy because Jesus Christ has made us free indeed. Are you living in that freedom, victory and joy each day? You can be assured by the words recorded in Romans 8:1-4, "There is now no condemnation for those who are in Christ Jesus, because through Christ Jesus the law of the Spirit who gives life has set you free from the law of sin and death." Since the Son has set you free, you are free indeed.

A contemporary hymn/song, "I Am Free" was written by Jon Egan from Desperation Band. The lyric expresses ways in which one is free indeed.

Through you the blind will see;
Through you the mute will sing;
Through you the dead will rise;
Through you all hearts will praise;
Through you the darkness flees;
Through you my heart screams -
I am free! Yes, I am free!

I am free to run;
I am free to dance;
I am free to live for You, I am free!

11. Consecrate Me Now

> Therefore, with minds that are alert and fully sober, set your hope on the grace to be brought to you when Jesus Christ is revealed at his coming. As obedient children, do not conform to the evil desires you had when you lived in ignorance. But just as he who called you is holy, so be holy in all you do; it is written: Be holy, because I am holy.
>
> First Peter 1:13-16 (NIV)

When God stipulated that a Tabernacle should be present in the midst of the people who had left Egypt, one important feature of the Tabernacle was the designated place called the Holy of Holies. It represented to the people that God was in their midst. It was not large in measurement (15' by 15') but was to be regarded as a sacred place because the presence of Jehovah God was there. There was no external light to illuminate the holy of holies because the presence of God's glory was there. There was no seat for man. Jehovah sat alone on the throne of glory, righteousness and mercy. Only the high priest was allowed to enter once a year. He would enter with bowed head, bare feet, and bells on his garment. No human voice was ever heard because it was only the voice of God that would be spoken and heard. The same structural function and requirement prevailed when the Temple was built by Solomon. While there is no structural temple, the spiritual application observes there is no need for a physical location to which the people of God would be required to go. The change that has occurred is stated in II Corinthians 6:17, "For we are the temple of the living God." We need to give serious consideration to what is meant for those who are designated as the Temple of the Living God.

I Chronicles 21 – 29 is an interesting study in the life of David, the things he did and wanted to do, and his needed acceptance of God's will versus his own will. In the midst of that study, as resources are being gathered and preparations are being made for the construction of the Temple, David asks a necessary and crucial question (I Chronicles 29:5), "Now who is willing to consecrate themselves to the Lord today?" In terms of consecration, I believe the first and last words of the question need to be underscored. The first word is "now" and the last word is "today." It is so easy to assume a status before the Lord or to procrastinate making an immediate affirmation. The infamous cliché is: "I'll get around to it." That cliché has become so common that a round piece of wood or some inexpensive metal about the size of a half-dollar is distributed as a "round-tuit"! To the above question about consecration, how should one answer that question and call? How vital is that challenge to consecration for you? How have you answered it?

This call for consecration was to impact and infiltrate one's life and all his efforts. When the children of Israel were standing at the threshold to the promised land, there was a time for instruction and preparation before moving toward or entering the land. Those words of instruction and preparation are given in Joshua 3:1-5,

> *"Early in the morning Joshua and all the Israelites set out and went to the Jordan, where they camped before crossing over. After three days, the officers went throughout the camp, giving orders to the people: When you see the ark of the covenant of the Lord your God, and the Levitical priests carrying it, you are to move out from your positions and follow it. Then you will know which way to go, since you have never been this way before."*

Joshua then told the people: Consecrate yourselves, for tomorrow the Lord will do amazing things among you." The key to their movement was to fully recognize that The Ark of the Covenant represented the presence of God in their midst. When the Levitical priests move out carrying The Ark – (carrying God) – Follow It. In following The Ark of God, the people will be assured of the Lord's guidance for them. Joshua 3:4 underscores the reality of this venture and need for divine guidance, "You will know which way to go, since you have never been this way before." To become lost and misdirected in a place where one is a stranger would be disconcerting. To have a Guide who knows the way would provide assurance and confidence. It also serves to remind us of our special relationship to and in Jesus Christ. The words of Psalm 23:1-3, are reassuring to all who can say and mean: "The Lord is my shepherd, I lack nothing. He makes me lie down in green pastures, He leads me beside quiet waters, He refreshes my soul. He guides me along the right paths for his name's sake." The emphasis points of these verses are the Shepherd knows and cares for the sheep's well-being; the Shepherd finds the very best place where He causes His sheep to lie down in green pastures; and the Shepherd wants the sheep to experience His comfort and peace as He leads them beside quiet and still waters. It is at such a place and in such an atmosphere that the Shepherd can and will cause His sheep refreshment for their weary souls. Fear and uncertainty is removed because the Shepherd knows the correct way and guides His sheep along the right and safe paths.

Part of the genius in The Shepherd's selection process is the plan and process He has for each one of His sheep. When it pertained to the special task He had in mind as He called disciples, He said. Matthew 4:19, "Come, follow me and I will send you out to fish for people." When Jesus emphasized he was the Good Shepherd, He said, John 10:27,

"My sheep listen to my voice; I know them, and they follow me." We need to note and observe the characteristic of the Shepherd's sheep. They listen to and for His voice. They learn and know intimacy with the Shepherd because He makes it His goal to know them so that they will know and trust Him instinctively and implicitly. Another indicator that is required in this intimate relationship is that the sheep follow and are guided by the Shepherd. An obvious question for the professing Christian: How well do you listen? What impresses you most about the Shepherd and gets your attention? Do we sometimes erect barriers to prevent us from observing and listening to the Shepherd? Like Adam and Eve in the Garden of Eden, do we have our moments where we try to hide from God because of some wrongdoing in our life?

An example to consider is the life of Elijah. In I Kings 18, Elijah has been involved in a contest with the prophets of Baal. The issue is about whose object of worship results in actual worship of the true God. The contest is agreed upon and the prophets of Baal fail in their effort to prove their god is viable and more powerful. When Elijah appeals to the only true God, the water-soaked offering is consumed by a fire, as well as the altar on which the sacrifice had been placed. The 450 prophets of Baal are slain and the people acknowledge that The Lord, He is God. Shortly after this great miracle and victory, Jezebel lets her sense of disappointment be known and proceeds to threaten to have Elijah killed. When he hears of her plan, he flees from the area and runs as quickly as he can to escape her impending threat upon his life. It was approximately a forty-day journey in his effort to escape the death threat upon his life. Elijah had run in fear. How will the Lord deal with Elijah and his fears? What will He do to gain the attention of Elijah? The Lord seeks him and calls him to come out of his hiding place. Elijah had found a cave where he felt safe and protected. However, the Lord knew where he was and summons Elijah out of his hiding place (I Kings 19:11-

13). The Lord said, "Go out and stand on the mountain in the presence of the Lord, for the Lord is about to pass by." The prophet is already fearful lest Jezebel finds where he is and seizes him. He knows that will mean instant death at her decree. The Lord will utilize four attention-getting means with Elijah. First, as soon as Elijah exits the cave and the Lord passes by, there is a great and powerful wind that tore the mountain apart and shattered the rocks. As impressive as that was, the Biblical text states: "but the Lord was not in the wind." Was Elijah disappointed? Fearful? Nonplussed?

Second, "After the wind there was an earthquake, but the Lord was not in the earthquake." Elijah had recently witnessed the great power of a Great God on Mount Carmel. It would be easy to reach a conclusion that God was reaching out to him in a similar manner with a display of power over His creation. If not in the strong wind, He would surely be present in the demonstrative earthquake. This was not the case. God was not in the earthquake. Do you have times when you are fearful and confused? All you want is for someone – anyone – to reach out to assist and encourage you! Elijah had experienced a powerful miracle of God and could easily conclude that when the wind blew fiercest and the earth trembled most dramatically that God was present. He had to recognize a reality that God was not in the wind or earthquake.

Thirdly, "After the earthquake came a fire, but the Lord was not in the fire." Elijah must've been beside himself at this point. God had recently demonstrated His power with fire that consumed the sacrifice, the water that drenched it and the altar itself. Why is God not in the fire at this point? God had called him out of the cave where he hid for his personal safety. He heard God's Word to him to come out as He passed by! In his fear, discouragement and confusion, has Elijah come to a point where he is no longer connected to God? When you and I pray, do we always sense the presence of God with us and listening to us? The God who promised never to leave or forsake His own is beside you. He wants you to believe in Him and increase in awareness of His constant presence in your life. Are you confident of these truths amid your fears and apprehensions?

Fourthly, "After the fire came a gentle whisper." Are you sensitive to the gentle whispers of God to you? When you seek Him, do you keep talking or do you pause to listen? Do you believe that when you are at your wits end, God's plan for your life is unaltered? At such intervals in our lives, we can and should be reassured that He has a good plan for our lives and is up to something that exceeds our expectations or anticipations. When Elijah heard the gentle whisper of God, he pulled his cloak over his face and went out and stood at the mouth of the cave. It is at this point that one would expect a spectacular miracle to occur that would lift Elijah up and take him to a new place where he would feel safe. God's plan and purpose was much different. The gentle voice of God was: "What are you doing here, Elijah?" That was not what he expected to hear? When you listen for the gentle whisper of God, what do you expect him to say to you? Are you eager to respond affirmatively to that gentle whisper or have you dictated to God the answer you want Him to grant?

Elijah received simple and basic instruction from the Lord, I Kings 19:11-16. The Lord said to him: "Go back the way you came." God knows all about Jezebel and her threats. God also knows all about Elijah's fears and reluctance to be anywhere near Jezebel. God will indicate to Elijah that he has unfinished business he needs to do, not sometime in the future - but now. Where is he to go and what has he left undone? God gently whispers to him: "Go to the Desert of Damascus. Anoint Hazael king over Aram. Also, Anoint Jehu king over Israel, and anoint Elisha to succeed you as prophet."

In the lives of many people, there are times when they feel unwanted and incapable. They believe they have nothing and unable to do anything constructive. This is true in terms of physical relationships. An area that produces considerable concern and tension is in the area of finances. The combination of frustration, helplessness, fatigue and emotional exhaustion are overwhelming. There can be those moments when one is frustrated and disappointed with God Himself. Where is He when I need Him so badly in my life right now? Has He forgotten me? What happened to His supplying for my needs? Where is He with the assurance that I need to get me through these circumstances in my life? Where is the Shepherd who will lead and guide me into green pastures and beside the still, peaceful waters?

I can remember vividly when our children were young and had some concerns about which they were disturbed. When one of them would rant on, their Mother would place her hands on their cheeks and have them look directly to her as she said: Listen to me! It was at such a moment she would share godly wisdom with them in the hope it would calm their immediate concerns or fears. Would there be other moments similar in their lives? Yes! What would be the loving action and godly expression to them? Her hands on their cheeks and her words to them: "Listen to me!" What happens when we don't listen to or anticipate the gentle whisper of God?

In this discourse with the Lord, Elijah seeks to justify why he has run to the cave and why is fearful to return. He has his list: I am the only prophet left; I have rendered tireless service; and now, I face death because of my faith and practice (I Kings 19). One can become myopic, self-absorbed so easily and allow the thought that I am all alone in this battle and ministry. The Lord states both a rebuke and reminder, (I Kings 19:18), "I will leave 7,000 in Israel, all the knees of whom have not bowed to Baal and every mouth that has not kissed him." These words are summarized by Paul in Romans 11:1-6,

> "I ask then, did God reject His people? Certainly not! I am an Israelite myself, a descendant of Abraham, from the tribe of Benjamin. God did not reject His people,

> whom He foreknew. Do you not know what the Scripture says about Elijah, how he appealed to God against Israel: Lord, they have killed Your prophets and torn down Your altars. I am the only one left, and they are seeking my life as well? And what was the divine reply to him? I have reserved for Myself seven thousand men who have not bowed the knee to Baal. In the same way, at the present time there is a remnant chosen by grace. And if it is by grace, then it is no longer by works. Otherwise, grace would no longer be grace."

It cannot be emphasized too often or stated too loudly that it is the grace of God that allows one to become unchained and to be free indeed. With this as our reality, we should enthusiastically respond to the Lord:

Consecrate me now, to Thy service, Lord,
By the power of grace divine;
Let my soul look up with a steadfast hope,
And my will be lost in Thine.
- Fanny J. Crosby –

Now who is willing to consecrate himself/herself to the Lord today? Can the Lord count on you as one of His unchained and free indeed followers? He's eager to have an intimate relationship with you as you walk and live in His presence.

12. Promises

May the God of endurance and encouragement grant you to live in such harmony with one another, in accord with Christ Jesus, that together you may with one voice glorify the God and Father of our Lord Jesus Christ. Therefore welcome one another as Christ has welcomed you, for the glory of God. For I tell you that Christ became a servant to the circumcised to show God's truthfulness, in order to confirm the promises given to the patriarchs, and in order that the gentiles might glorify God for his mercy. May the God of hope fill you with all joy and peace in believing, so that by the power of the Holy Spirit you may abound in hope.

(Romans 15:5-9, 13)

But as surely as God is faithful, our message to you is not yes and no. For the Son of God, Jesus Christ, who was proclaimed among you…was not yes and no, but in Him it has always been yes. For all the promises of God are yes in Christ. And so through Him, our Amen is spoken to the glory of God.

(Second Corinthians 1:18-20)

What is a promise? Generally, it is accepted as: A "pledge, vow, a guarantee, or an assurance." In a court room, one who is called upon to give testimony about an event, person or deed is asked to "swear to tell the truth, the whole truth, and nothing but the truth, so help me God." Failure to keep this oath or misrepresenting the truth has negative results, including perjury (giving of false evidence); subject to a fine or penalty; and the possibility of incarceration.

When a couple is married, there is a marriage vow taken where the man and woman indicate they will, "love, honor and cherish until death us do part." Sadly, the number of marriages ending in divorce would indicate it is a sacred vow and promise not always kept. Politicians seeking public office fill their speeches with a variety of promises they will enact if you elect them to a particular office. How has that worked out so far in the national politics of the United States? The low approval rating for elected individuals is an indicator that trust has been violated and promises made have not been promises kept. It would serve politicians well if they observed some quotes about promises. Some quotes regarding promises attributed to notable people include: "We must not promise what we ought not, lest we be called on to perform what we cannot" (Abraham Lincoln). Another is: "Promises are like crying babies in a theater, they should be carried out at once" (Norman Vincent Peale).

When it comes to the professing Christian and the Church organization, how many promises made and expected to be embraced are there in the bible (66 books)? Depending on the translation being used, the estimated range is from approximately 3,000 to 8,000 promises made. One unnamed person who used the King James Version of the Bible determined there were 3,573 promises in the Holy Scriptures. The first promise after the fall is Genesis 3:15 that addresses the ongoing spiritual conflict and warfare because of the fall of mankind. The text indicates: "So the Lord God said to the serpent: I will put enmity between you and the woman, and between your offspring and hers; He will crush your head, and you will strike his heel." The last promise in the Word of God pertains to the end of all spiritual conflict and warfare. The text is Revelation 22:12-21 (selected): "The message of Jesus from heaven and spoken by the angel:

> Look, I am coming soon! My reward is with me, and I will give to each person according to what they have

> done. I am the Alpha and the Omega, the first and the last, the beginning and the end. I, Jesus, have sent my angel to give you this testimony for the churches…The spirit and the bride say, come! And let the one who hears say, come! Let the one who is thirsty come; and let the one who wishes take the free gift of the water of life. He who testifies to these things says, yes, I am coming soon. Amen. Come, Lord Jesus. The grace of the Lord Jesus be with God's people. Amen.

In between the first promise and last promise in Scripture, several centuries have taken place. In that historical time-frame, there have been murders, wars, threats of war, people in bondage, elongated periods of captivity, persecution, corruption and Crucifixion. That which prevails through all historic periods are God's unfailing promises. You should find encouragement and consolation in the words of Second Peter 1:3-4,

> His divine power has given us everything we need for a godly life through our knowledge of Him who called us by His own glory and goodness. Through these He has given us his very great and precious promises, so that through them you may participate in the divine nature, having escaped the corruption in the world caused by evil desires.

Despite what may be occurring in the world at any given point and time, focus on the words: "He has given us his very great and precious promises, so that through them you may participate in the divine nature." An ongoing gift of God's grace is His very great and precious promises. Regardless of any counted number, all of the promises are validated in Jesus Christ for those who believe in Him.

A question that should be pondered is: Are God's promises conditional or unconditional? To answer that question satisfactorily, we consult the Word of God to determine that which is required so that God's promises can become validated in each life. Second Corinthians 6:14 through 7:1 lays the foundational premises for us. To glean God's requirement, we begin with Second Corinthians 7:1, "Since we have these promises, dear friends, let us purify ourselves from everything that contaminates body and spirit, perfecting holiness out of reverence for God."

Let us consider once again: Are God's promises unconditional or conditional? Does God have any expectation for his people? If so, what are His expectations? The answer is that God's expectation for His people includes that we are: "Purifying ourselves from everything that contaminates body and spirit; that we are pursuing and actively perfecting holiness; and we are always maintaining reverence for God."

What does purifying – perfecting – reverencing require? In part, it requires a serious assessment of one's personal spiritual life and the choices being made. It would include pondering the words of Second Corinthians 6:14-16, "Do not be yoked together with unbelievers." The immediate focus would be on what this directive includes and implies. It must be responded to transparently and correctly. Paul utilizes a series of questions, using contrasts for clarification. He stated: "For what do righteousness and wickedness have in common? Or what fellowship can light have with darkness? What harmony (agreement) is there between Christ and Belial (the spirit of evil personified; the devil; Satan)**?** What does a believer have in common with an unbeliever? What agreement is there between the temple of god and idols?" There can be no adaptation or compromise with these contrasts. It is obvious that a choice must be made between the contrasts. The action of purifying, perfecting and reverencing requires understanding and accepting who and what we are in God's sight. Paul goes on to state that which should govern our responses: "We are the temple of the living

God." At the very least, the idea of The Temple should represent to us that the presence of God is in the midst of The Temple and His glory is filling this holy place. This is who and what we are supposed to be for God and before Him. His presence is both with us and within us. His glory is to be dominant in our lives and radiate from us.

Paul shares not only the requirement for God's people, he also shares the reality for the life of we who are The Temple of the Living God. We begin to learn the heart of God for and toward His people. It harks back to the Garden of Eden and the intimacy there was with Adam and Eve each day. What God wanted there He wants now with each one who names His name. Paul continues, "As God has said (promised): I will live with them; I will walk among them; I will be their God; They will be my people," That which God requires for those desiring the reality of His promises in their lives is clearly stated in specific terms and conditions: "Come out from them,

be separate and touch no unclean thing." As this is enacted upon in the life of each believer, the Lord Almighty is committed to additional promises: "I will receive you. I will be a father to you, You will be My sons and daughters." This becomes the restoration of a unique and precious relationship with God that God wants daily fellowship with His people.

It is followed by the grand finale summary in Second Corinthians 7:1, "Therefore, since we have these promises, dear friends, let us purify ourselves from everything that contaminates body and spirit." We are to act positively upon that which God has stipulated. All of His promises are readily available for all who will obey and comply with His directives. It entails our action as stipulated in verse 17, "Come out; Be separate; Avoid touching that which is unclean." Why? Because we are to consciously and deliberately seeking to implement: "Let us perfect holiness out of reverence for God." There are sufficient reminders in

God's Word in this regard. We gain further clarity about "perfecting holiness" in Hebrews 12:14, "Make every effort to live in peace with everyone and to be holy; without holiness no one will see the Lord."

Is your faith and hope based upon the very great and precious promises of God? Are you standing on the promises of God every day? Do you claim the provision of Jesus Christ to be free indeed?

There are Gospel promises you can rely upon. One is John 6:37, "All those the Father gives me will come to me, and whoever comes to me I will never drive away (never cast out)." Another is in John 5:24, "Truly, I say to you, he who hears my word, and believes him who sent me, has eternal life, and does not come into judgment, but has passed out of death into life." There is the word of assurance in John 10:27-28, "My sheep listen to my voice, I know them and they follow me. I give them eternal life and they will never perish. No one can snatch them out of my hand." Among the hundreds and thousands of promises in God's Word, there is always the assurance that God is faithful and He cares for His own. Some promises that should encourage you along your journey of life include: Philippians 4:19, "but my God shall supply all your need according to his riches in glory by Christ Jesus." Second Corinthians 12:9, God has promised that his grace is sufficient for us. In Jeremiah 29:11 and Romans 8:28, there is the reminder that God is working all things according to His eternal plan for our temporal good. As we progress on our life's journey, He acknowledges there will be times of challenge, and He has promised that, First Corinthians 10:13, his children will not be overtaken with temptation because He will make a way of escape for us.

The calculated estimate of the total number of promises are between 3,000 to 8,000. The precise total should not concern us too greatly because we are given this assurance in Second Corinthians 1:20, "For no matter how many promises

God has made, they are "Yes" in Christ. And so through him the Amen is spoken by us to the glory of God." We can confidently say that if there are ten or ten thousand promises, in Christ, they are all declared to be "Yes" for all of God's children all of the time. Being free indeed gives you the right to stand upon and personally claim the promises of God for you. In 1886, R. Keslo Carter penned these words (Stanza 4):

Standing on the promises I cannot fall,
Listening every moment to the Spirit's call
Resting in my Savior as my all in all,
Standing on the promises of God.

Positionally, if you are Standing On The Promises Of God each day of your life, you should know the full extent of being unchained and being free indeed. The promises of God are foundational for us and should bolster our spiritual being so that we can walk humbly and joyously with the Lord.

13. Oaths and Vows

> Walk prudently when you go to the house of God; and draw near to hear rather than to give the sacrifice of fools, for they do not know that they do evil. Do not be rash with your mouth, And let not your heart utter anything hastily before God. For God is in heaven, and you on earth; Therefore, let your words be few…When you make a vow to God, do not delay to pay it; For He has no pleasure in fools. Pay what you have vowed. Better not to vow than to vow and not pay.
>
> Ecclesiastes 5:1-5 (NKJV)

Within the contemporary culture, oaths and vows are not taken very seriously. This is observable across the culture in the United States of America. It is illustrated by protests and riots that often denigrate the government and desecrate the American Flag. It is obvious there is little appreciation for a nation that is founded upon liberty and justice for all. There was a time when people who had opportunity of returning to America, when they disembarked from a plane or ship, would immediately kneel down and kiss the ground. In days gone by, immigrants to this nation were funneled through Ellis Island in New York Harbor. They looked forward to becoming a part of this nation with untold and unlimited opportunities for them.

On a personal basis, my family was very proud when a teenage orphan who had been adopted in Ukraine by my son's family became a citizen of the United States of America. She smiled broadly and the small American Flag she had been given was waved proudly and enthusiastically by her. But first, the United States Citizenship and Immigration Services required the following Oath to be taken:

> I hereby declare, on oath, that I absolutely and entirely renounce and abjure all allegiance and fidelity to any foreign prince, potentate, state, or sovereignty of whom or which I have heretofore been a subject or citizen; that I will support and defend the Constitution and laws of the United States of America against all enemies, foreign and domestic; that I will bear true faith and allegiance to the same; that I will bear arms on behalf of the United States when required by law; that I will perform noncombatant service in the Armed Forces of the United States when required by the law; that I will perform work of national importance under civilian direction when required by the law; and that I take this obligation freely without any mental reservation or purpose of evasion; so help me God.
>
> In acknowledgement whereof I have hereunto affixed my signature.

Not only has our Granddaughter assimilated into an American Family and Church, she has also worked diligently to learn English and to develop communication skills. When she first arrived, communication was almost impossible. She spoke no English and our family spoke neither Russian or Ukrainian. At this writing, Julia has been working with the Bridge of Faith Ministry in Alabama and their efforts with orphans from Ukraine. She is able to be a translator-communicator for this group. She has also become part of the team that travels periodically to Ukraine. It is a special joy to hear Julia refer to our son and his wife as Dad and Mom, as well as to my wife and me as Grandma and Grandpa. It reminds us of the meaningful words about adoption by the Apostle Paul in Galatians 4:4-6,

> But when the fullness of the time had come, God sent forth His Son, born of a woman, born under the law, to

> redeem those who were under the law, that we might receive the adoption as sons (daughters). And because you are sons (daughters), God has sent forth the Spirit of His Son into your hearts, crying out, Abba, Father! Therefore, you are no longer a slave but a son, and if a son (daughter), then an heir of God through Christ.

As part of the emphasis above in Galatians 4:4-6, the suggestion is obvious that one has not been made into an island unto itself but incorporated into a spiritual family. The natural thing one should strive toward is to become an interactional part of the spiritual family. Some never do. Others who have identified with a group have failed to meet commitments and obligations to the spiritual family. The oath taken for Church Membership and the seriousness with which the vows are taken may vary from group to group. In my denominational affiliation, the minimum requirement and expectation for Church Membership is fivefold:

1. Do you acknowledge yourself to be a sinner in the sight of God, justly deserving His displeasure, and without hope save in His sovereign mercy?
2. Do you believe in the Lord Jesus Christ as the Son of God, and Savior of sinners, and do you receive and rest upon Him alone for salvation as He is offered in the Gospel?
3. Do you now resolve and promise, in humble reliance upon the grace of the Holy Spirit, that you will endeavor to live as becomes the followers of Christ?
4. Do you promise to support the Church in its worship and work to the best of your ability?
5. Do you submit yourself to the government and discipline of the Church, and promise to study its purity and peace?

Sadly, and all too quickly, some ignore these vows and the commitments made. Does such a one have a reason or excuse? In their mind, they do. Are they demonstrating that they take these oaths and vows seriously? Strangely, the obvious response is that they have not taken them at all seriously. It is not just the oath and vow taken before a congregation that is being violated. In the more important way they are ignoring the Lord's directive and desire. First, there is the ignoring and infraction as it pertains to Exodus 20:8-11 (NASB),

> Remember the Sabbath Day, to keep it holy. Six days you shall labor and do all your work, but the seventh day is a Sabbath of the Lord your God; in it you shall not do any work, you or your son or your daughter, your male or your female servant or your cattle or your sojourner who stays with you. For in six days the Lord made the heavens and the earth, the sea and all that is in them, and rested on the seventh day; therefore, the Lord blessed the Sabbath Day and made it holy.

Do you take the Sabbath Day as seriously as God does? Do you regard it as a holy day that requires your commitment and positive response to worship the Lord on His Sabbath Day?

Secondly, the Psalmist viewed the Sabbath Day as a unique opportunity for corporate worship with those of like precious faith. This joyous anticipation and expectation is expressed by David in Psalm 122:1 (NASB), "I was glad when they said to me: Let us go to the house of the Lord." Do you have that joyous expectation as the Christian Sabbath approaches? Does your family see your eagerness to observe the Sabbath Day and to keep it holy? Are you firmly committed to worship the Lord with His people so that, unless providentially hindered, you will joyfully be there?

Thirdly, there is the hortatory directive in Hebrews 10:23-25 (NASB) that addresses the commitment required and the activity expected,

> Let us hold fast the confession of our hope without wavering, for He who promised is faithful; and let us consider how to stimulate one another to love and good deeds, not forsaking our own assembling together, as is the habit of some, but encouraging one another; and all the more as you see the day drawing near.

There are four expectations required: (1) Hold fast the confession of your hope without wavering; (2) Consider ways to stimulate others to model love and to be engaged in good deeds; (3) Be careful and guarded lest you neglect the obligatory privilege of assembling with those of like precious faith; and (4) Be an encourager so that others will also live up to and be in compliance with the expectations of God for His people.

Expectation One uses a phrase, "without wavering." Among the many possibilities, and at the very least, the directive is stating that one should guard against becoming unsteady or begin to fall away. It also connotes the feeling or show of doubt or indecision. James 1:5-8 (NASB), broadens the horizon of wavering or doubting when he wrote,

> But if any of you lacks wisdom, let him ask of God, who gives to all generously and without reproach, and it will be given to him. But he must ask in faith without any doubting, for the one who doubts is like the surf of the sea, driven and tossed by the wind. For that man ought not to expect that he will receive anything from the Lord, being a double-minded man, unstable in all his ways.

One of the subtle issues is whether or not one is aware of the need for wisdom versus double-mindedness. Knowing and admitting that need can become needlessly evasive. It causes one to wonder why communication with the Lord is so infrequent. Also, why we ignore and neglect the fact that God responds to those who ask generously and without reproach. One may be hesitant because of the inability to determine genuine needs as differentiated from miscalculated wants. The refuge one should claim and be confident in is that regardless of how we utter our request, we have the assurance of Romans 8:26-27 (NASB), "In the same way the Spirit also helps our weakness; for we do not know how to pray as we should, but the Spirit Himself intercedes for us with groaning too deep for words; and He who searches the hearts knows what the mind of the Spirit is, because He intercedes for the saints according to the will of God."

The basics for arriving at and receiving wisdom depends upon one's heart relationship to the Lord and the readiness for the will of God for one's life. In a general way, application should be made in our lives based upon Proverbs 1:1-7,

> The proverbs of Solomon the son of David, king of Israel: To know wisdom and instruction, to discern the sayings of understanding, to receive instruction in wise behavior, righteousness, justice and equity; to give prudence to the naive, To the youth knowledge and discretion, a wise man will hear and increase in learning, And a man of understanding will acquire wise counsel, to understand a proverb and a figure, the words of the wise and their riddles. The fear of the Lord is the beginning of knowledge; Fools despise wisdom and instruction.

The Apostle Paul offered an amplified prayer regarding wisdom in Ephesians 1:15-19,

> For this reason, ever since I heard about your faith in the Lord Jesus and your love for all the saints, I have

> not stopped giving thanks for you, remembering you in my prayers and asking that the God of our Lord Jesus Christ, the glorious Father, may give you a spirit of wisdom and revelation in your knowledge of Him. I ask that the eyes of your heart may be enlightened, so that you may know the hope of His calling, the riches of His glorious inheritance in the saints, and the surpassing greatness of His power to us who believe.

The bottom-line remains in terms of oaths and vows. Are you fastidious in your observance of the vows you have taken or are you slothful in your duties and obligations? A passage of Scripture that may have an unwanted analogy, even though it is applicable, is Proverbs 6:6-11,

Go to the ant, O sluggard, observe her ways and be wise, which, having no chief, Officer or ruler, prepares her food in the summer and gathers her provision in the harvest. How long will you lie down, O sluggard? When will you arise from your sleep? A little sleep, a little slumber, a little folding of the hands to rest - Your poverty will come in like a vagabond and your need like an armed man.

While the text is addressing the need for diligence in one's work ethic, there is an obvious spiritual application as well. It is present when Jesus spoke in the Parable of the Ten Virgins, Matthew 25:1-13. The subject matter pertains to the readiness and preparation for the coming of the Bridegroom. The passage indicates that five of the ten were lackadaisical and matter-of-fact with their commitment, expectation and preparation. As a result, at the crucial moment when the announcement of The Bridegroom's arrival was made known, it caused them panic. Their personal lack of preparation, coupled with their hollow expectation, caused them to ultimately miss the coming of the Bridegroom. Could that represent you and your spiritual commitment and expectation? Will you have sufficient oil for your lamp when The

Bridegroom suddenly arrives? Or, will you be filled with sorrow and regret rather than joy and gladness because you failed to take God seriously?

Phillip Doddridge (1702-1751) wrote challenging words that every lackadaisical soul should consider and embrace:

Awake, my soul, stretch every nerve,
And press with vigor on;
A heavenly race demands thy zeal,
And an immortal crown.

Many of us are able to stretch every nerve and press with vigor on. The question remains for us to answer, namely, are we ready and willing to exert ourselves in a worthy cause, or are we bound and chained by the traditions passed down to us by former and present generations? Are we reticent to take a bold and decisive stand because of secular tendencies within the structured and traditional church? Do we allow ourselves to become intimidated by those who are a stronger secular influence? Do we succumb to the political correctness or are we willing to run the risks and stand for spiritual principles, foundational truths and moral values?

We need to be unchained and unbound by the power of God so that we can do His bidding – and – to be free indeed! May the Lord grant that reality in our lives for His glory.

> Epaphras, who is one of you and a servant of Christ Jesus, sends you greetings. He is always wrestling in prayer for you, so that you may stand mature and fully assured in the full will of God. For I testify about him that he goes to great pains for you and for those at Laodicea and Hierapolis.
>
> Colossians 4:12-13

The letter to the Colossian Church highlights certain truths that ought to be implemented into people's lives and the Church of which they have become a viable part. The forceful truth in one's life and the Church attended is the avowed basic goal and purpose for both. Colossians 1:18 requires attention be given and commitment made to Jesus Christ "so that in everything he might be preeminent." For anyone to be preeminent requires that He has absolute first place and authority in all areas of one's life. It is to be Christ alone at all times and in all things. Why should Jesus Christ be preeminent? Why should He have first place and authority in all things at all times? The reason given in Colossians 1:16-17 is: "By him all things were created, in heaven and on earth, visible and invisible, whether thrones or dominions or rulers or authorities - all things were created through him and for him. And he is before all things, and in him all things hold together."

It is at this juncture that we first learn of the role of Epaphras and his labors. Paul observed what the Word of truth is accomplishing, Colossians 1:16-17,

> It is bearing fruit and increasing, as it also does among you, since the day you heard it and understood the grace of God in truth, just as you learned it from

> Epaphras our beloved fellow servant. He is a faithful minister of Christ on your behalf and has made known to us your love in the Spirit.

As was often the case, Paul was consistent in establishing the rightful place for the giving of thanks to the Lord because of His watch-care and provision for His people. Thanks-Giving and Thanks-Living are to be observable by all and implemented as quickly as possible in the lives of new adherents to the word of truth faithfully proclaimed. A few examples are:

Colossians 1:3, 11-12 - We always thank God, the Father of our Lord Jesus Christ, when we pray for you…Being strengthened with all power according to His glorious might so that you may have full endurance and patience, and joyfully giving thanks to the Father, who has qualified you to share in the inheritance of the saints in the light.

Colossians 2:6-7 - Just as you have received Christ Jesus as Lord, continue to live in Him, rooted and built up in Him, established in the faith as you were taught, and overflowing with thankfulness.

Colossians 3:15-16 - Let the peace of Christ rule in your hearts, for to this you were called as members of one body. And be thankful. Let the word of Christ richly dwell within you as you teach and admonish one another with all wisdom, and as you sing psalms, hymns, and spiritual songs with gratitude in your hearts to God.

Colossians 4:2 - Devote yourselves to prayer, being watchful and be thankful.

It reminds one to recall the words written by Andrea Crouch in his worship song, My Tribute:

How can I say thanks for the things You have done for me?
Things so undeserved, yet You gave to prove Your love for me;

the voices of a million angels could not express my gratitude.
All that I am and ever hope to be, I owe it all to Thee.
[Chorus1]
To God be the glory, to God be the glory,
to God be the glory
for the things He has done.
With His blood He has saved me, with His power
He has raised me;
to God be the glory for the things He has done.
Just let me live my life, let it pleasing, Lord to Thee,
and if I gain any praise, let it go to Calvary.
To God be the glory, to God be the glory,
to God be the glory for the things He has done.

The question for which there should be resolve is: How can one raise a high standard of watchfulness while maintain an equally high standard of thankfulness? Paul gives a twofold frontal approach to attain this standard. First is Colossians 4:2, prayerful watchfulness with thanksgiving, and Second is Colossians 4:12, being mature and fully assured in all the will of God. Paul shares some components to develop prayerful watchfulness with Thanks-giving so one will be better able to manifest Thanks-living.

One component is Colossians 4:5, walking in wisdom with outsiders. This will entail discipline so that one will be making the best use of time. It requires the need to avoid superfluous distractions (that which has little or nothing to do with one's relationship to Jesus Christ or becoming spiritually mature and being firmly committed to know and do all the will of God for one's life). Another superfluous distraction is one that would cause deviation from the commission and ministry tasks.

A second component appears in Colossians 4:6, one's speech must always be gracious. Webster's revised unabridged dictionary defines being gracious as: "abounding in grace or mercy; manifesting love; bestowing mercy; characterized by grace; disposed to show kindness or favor; amiability." The International Standard Bible Encyclopedia expands on the basic definition. It states: "being gracious contains two evident shades of meaning: (1) It is favorable or causative; to cause to be gracious. It cites as its meaning, Numbers 6:24-26, The Aaronic Benediction phrase that expresses: "May the Lord make his face to shine upon thee and be gracious unto thee." Being gracious also includes the statement of fact, Psalm 145:8, "The Lord is gracious and full of compassion." The word is used once in the New Testament, I Peter 2:3, (from the root of the Greek word chrestos): being useful as a benefit - "If you have tasted that the Lord is gracious." In the OT, it is applied to Jehovah as indicative of His favor and mercy, His long-suffering and general inclination of favor and kindness. A third component is given in Colossians 4:7-8 where one is enjoined to be encouraged as well as being an encourager. Paul wrote: "Tychicus will tell you all about my activities. He is a beloved brother and faithful minister and fellow servant in the Lord. I have sent him to you for this very purpose, that you may know how we are and that he may encourage your hearts."

What does encouragement mean and what does it entail? At the very least, it is action of giving someone support, confidence, or hope. It is also the act of trying to stimulate the development of an activity, state, or belief. The Biblical application is clearly stated in First Thessalonians 5:11, "Therefore encourage one another and build one another up, just as you are doing." Additionally, in Hebrews 10:23-25 we read about encouragement in a broader application,

> Let us hold fast the confession of our hope without wavering, for he who promised is faithful. And let us consider how to stir up one another to love and good works, not neglecting to meet together, as is the habit

of some, but encouraging one another, and all the more as you see the Day drawing near.

The relevancy of the words in Hebrews 10:23-25 is the basis of the devotional, Get More Strength for The Journey by Joseph Stowell, – November 18, 2017,

> Douglas Coupland is a best-selling author known for his books about cultural trends in America. In his book Life After God, he no doubt surprises his readers when he shares:
>
> Now here is my secret. I tell it to you with an openness of heart I doubt I will ever achieve again . . . My secret is that I need God—that I am sick and can no longer make it alone. I need God to help me give, because I no longer seem to be capable of giving; to help me be kind, as I no longer seem capable of kindness; to help me love, as I seem beyond being able to love.
>
> Amazing! An author who has admittedly bought into the godless secularism in our world has let his godless philosophy of life run its course, and at the end of it all he recognizes that something is missing. The unanswered longing in his soul leads him to admit that his "life after God" has left him barren and hopelessly in need. He calls it his secret because it would be almost scandalous in post-Christian America to admit that we do need God after all, the God who has been banished to the outposts of irrelevance.

An additional poignant reminder about one's need for God is Ecclesiastes 3:10-11, 14.

> I have seen the business that God has given to the children of man to be busy with. He has made everything beautiful in its time. Also, He has put eternity into man's heart, yet so that he cannot find out

> what God has done from the beginning to the end. I perceived that whatever God does endures forever; nothing can be added to it, nor anything taken from it. God has done it, so that people fear before him.

A point of clarification of the words and phrases in Hebrews 10:23-25: "Stirring Up" does not mean strife or argument. Its focus is on edification. It conveys the goal for improvement of a person morally or intellectually. The term "Encouraging" is in the context of fellowship and worship. There is a sense of urgency attached: "And all the more as you see the day approaching." The day refers to the moment when the Bridegroom returns for His Bride, the Church. This echoes the same words in Colossians 2:1-3 where Paul wrote:

> For I want you to know how great a struggle I have for you and for those at Laodicea and for all who have not seen me face to face, that their hearts may be encouraged, being knit together in love, to reach all the riches of full assurance of understanding and the knowledge of God's mystery, which is Christ, in whom are hidden all the treasures of wisdom and knowledge.

The words in Colossians 4:12 have always had special meaning and application. It is a picture of Epaphras working with and praying for the people of the Colossian Church. The heart expression of Epaphras is that each person in the Church will become a spiritually mature person. It is assumed that Epaphras serves in the role of a Pastor to the people. Some commentators suggest he might even have been an Evangelist. The text states about Epaphras: "who is one of you and a servant of Christ Jesus." It is an example of cohesiveness, rather than fractional, within the body of believers. Epaphras projects that he is ready and willing to do whatever is needed to be done for and with the people of God. The commitment of

Epaphras and the scope of his concern for the Church is stated as: “He is always wrestling in prayer for you.” Part of his focus and concern is expressed in his purpose: “that you may stand mature and fully assured in the full will of God.” Paul would write his observation of this dear servant of the Lord: “For I testify about him that he goes to great pains for you and for those at Laodicea and Hierapolis.” Paul shares that Epaphras exerts himself for the cause of Christ and the precious flock(s) entrusted to his care.”

How does the prayer of Epaphras apply to the Church today? How does it apply to the people of God today? The application is given in Colossians 4:12, to become a fully assured spiritual person. Fully assured solidifies who one is in and through Jesus Christ. It is also a reminder of what one has because of Jesus Christ. How does one know the reality and truths regarding these things? Romans 8:16-17 assures one:

> The Spirit Himself testifies with our spirit that we are God’s children. And if we are children, then we are heirs: heirs of God and co-heirs with Christ, if indeed we suffer with Him, so that we may also be glorified with Him.

Colossians 4:12 also indicates that one can be confident in all the will of God. The question that often arises is: How can one get to know the will of God? A starting point would be Proverbs 3:5-6, “Trust in the Lord with all your heart and lean not on your own understanding; in all your ways submit to him (acknowledge), and he will make your paths straight (He will direct your paths).” To know the will of God necessitates making a choice and confirming it with a deliberate, not a frivolous or emotional, commitment. Romans 12:1-2 instructs: “Do not be conformed to this world but be transformed by the renewing of your mind. Then you will be able to discern what is the good, pleasing, and perfect will of God.”

Evangeline Vergo (Campus Crusade For Christ), has written a practical paper on: How To Know The Will of God. It begins with enjoinder: Getting A Grip On Guidance. The steps suggested include:

1) Surrender your attitude and personal desires. Think through why you would want to make a certain choice. Are your desires in alignment with God's desires?

2) Meditate on God's Word. When you make a decision, it should line up with, or at least not contradict, what God has already said through the Bible.

3) Spend focused time in prayer. God tells us: "Do not be anxious about anything, but in everything, by prayer and petition, with thanksgiving, present your requests to God" (Philippians 4:6, NIV). As you ask God what to do, write down the sense of direction you get from Him over time.

4) Seek other people's opinions. Find mature, dedicated Christians and ask them what they think you should do. The opinions you receive may conflict, but they should give you another perspective to think about.

5) Consider your circumstances. God can open and close opportunities. God, not circumstances, should guide your decision-making.

6) Think through your decision logically. God's Spirit can/will direct your mind and reasoning.

One of the problems for those who are chained and shackled because of negative choices is the obvious restriction one must endure. While chained and shackled, it is impossible to be fully assured in all the will of God. There is only one way to become unchained and unshackled, and that is in and by the grace and mercy of Jesus Christ. It is only by Him that anyone can know what it means to be free indeed. Once the issue of being free indeed is a reality, there is Biblical application of what has taken place in one's life. A clear description of what it means to be free indeed is given in Titus 2:11-14,

> For the grace of God has appeared, bringing salvation to all men. It instructs us to renounce ungodliness and worldly passions, and to live sensible, upright, and godly lives in the present age, http://biblehub.com/titus/2-13.htm as we await the blessed hope and glorious appearance of our great God and Savior, Jesus Christ. He gave Himself for us to redeem us from all lawlessness and to purify for Himself a people for His own possession, zealous for good deeds.

After the reality and presence of the race of God in one's life, God has given basic instructions and directions in His Word regarding His will and that which pleases Him - - -

I Thessalonians 5:18 – Give Thanks in all circumstances, for this is God's Will for you.

First Peter 2:15 – For it is God's will that by doing good you should silence the ignorance of foolish men

First Thessalonians 4:3-5 - For it is God's will that you should be holy: You must abstain from sexual immorality; each of you must know how to control his own body in holiness and honor, not in lustful passion…

First Corinthians 2:14-16 - The natural person does not accept the things of the Spirit of God, for they are folly to him, and he is not able to understand them because they are spiritually discerned…For who has understood the mind of the Lord so as to instruct him? But we have the mind of Christ.

Someone (Unknown Person) Observed: "As we walk with the Lord, obeying His Word and relying on His Spirit, we find that we are given the mind of Christ. When receiving the mind of Christ – We also gain the knowledge of God's Will."

The more we know Jesus Christ will help and enable us to know His will. One's goal for life must be: To know Him and to make Him known. God's guidance will be readily available for the sincere person with a seeking heart. Proverbs

11:5-6 instructs, "The righteousness of the blameless keeps his way straight, but the wicked falls by his own wickedness. The righteousness of the upright delivers them, but the treacherous are taken captive by their lust."

One's Prayer/Hymn from the heart should be: O To Be Like Thee – By: Thomas O. Chisholm.

O to be like Thee! blessed Redeemer,
This is my constant longing and prayer;
Gladly I'll forfeit all of earth's treasures,
Jesus, Thy perfect likeness to wear.

O to be like Thee! full of compassion,
Loving, forgiving, tender and kind,
Helping the helpless, cheering the fainting,
Seeking the wandering sinner to find.

For those who have been unchained and set free indeed should be prayerfully watching and waiting for The Bridegrooms return. While doing so, one should continue serving and being thankful. Paul wrote, First Timothy 1:12, "I thank Christ Jesus our Lord, who has strengthened me, that He considered me faithful and appointed me to service." To the end that we will know Him and His will and endeavoring to make Him known wherever one is located. Does this describe who you are? Does it represent where you are positionally as a Biblical Christian? Let it be known to all by your Thanks-giving and modelled by your Thanks-living.

15. My Identification

> According to my earnest expectation and hope that in nothing I shall be ashamed, but with all boldness, as always, so now also Christ will be magnified in my body, whether by life or by death. For to me, to live is Christ, and to die is gain. But if I live on in the flesh, this will mean fruit from my labor; yet what I shall choose I cannot tell. For I am hard-pressed between the two, having a desire to depart and be with Christ, which is far better. Nevertheless to remain in the flesh is more needful for you. And being confident of this, I know that I shall remain and continue with you all for your progress and joy of faith, that your rejoicing for me may be more abundant in Jesus Christ by my coming to you again.
>
> Philippians 1:20-27 (Selected – NKJV)

Basic questions one should ask: How would I identify myself? What do I do secularly and spiritually? Which one gets my greatest attention and amount of time – the secular or the spiritual? What is the chief concern I have presently? How would I like to be identified? How do I want to be remembered? There are many ways these questions can be answered but narrowing it down to a brief sentence/phrase of five words or less, what would you say or write?

A suggested list for the Biblical Christian is given in the Beatitudes (Matthew 5): "I am meek! I am poor in spirit. I am humble! I am merciful! I hunger/thirst for righteousness! I am pure in heart!" Some would deem that to be presumptive, fanatical or dodging the question! Is it presumptive or fanatical to follow the teachings of Jesus Christ? Why is there a suggestion that these phrases are dodging the question? What question is being dodged? Isn't the summary of the

Beatitudes precisely summarize That which Jesus was teaching and requiring of His followers? Does he require anything less than that today? Why is one hesitant or reluctant to respond to Him and His teaching? Psalm 107:2 (NASB) reminds one, "Let the redeemed of the Lord say so, Whom He has redeemed from the hand of the adversary." Isn't that who and what you/we are? Isn't that one's true identity in Jesus Christ - Redeemed by the blood of the Lamb - Jesus Christ and made a new creation in/by Him? Yes!

Our song and testimony should be the words written by Fanny Crosby,

Redeemed—how I love to proclaim it!
Redeemed by the blood of the Lamb;
Redeemed through His infinite mercy,
His child, and forever, I am.

A broader question arises when one is confronted with adversity. How does one respond or react at such times? A testimony about a devastating moment is shared in A Story About A Hymn (New Life Bible Presbyterian Church; January22, 2017). Some of the detail is: "In 1978, cancer was discovered in Ron Hamilton's left eye. Many people in his circumstance would be emotionally devastated and cave in, yield to self-pity or even leave the faith. Although Ron and his wife Shelly never fully understood why God allowed him to go through this ordeal, they committed everything to God's gracious hand and let His will be done. He said, Hearing a doctor say I had cancer and may die was a very sobering experience. Many people would see the loss of my eye and the need for wearing a patch as a great trial. But I see it as one of the greatest blessings of my life. It reminds me that God teaches us the greatest lessons in the deepest valleys. Immediately after the loss of his eye due to cancer, Ron Hamilton penned a song based on Philippians 4:4, which says: "Rejoice in the Lord always; again, I will say, rejoice."

Our renewed perspective and purpose for life could also be song in the words of the Hymn: O, Rejoice in the Lord. The lyrics include:

God never moves without purpose or plan
When trying His servant and molding a man.
Give thanks to the Lord though your testing seems long;
In darkness He giveth a song.

I could not see through the shadows ahead;
So I looked at the cross of my Savior instead.
I bowed to the will of the Master that day;
Then peace came and tears fled away.

Now I can see testing comes from above;
God strengthens His children and purges in love.
My Father knows best, and I trust in His care;
Through purging more fruit I will bear.

Refrain:

O Rejoice in the Lord He makes no mistake,
He knoweth the end of each path that I take,
For when I am tried And purified,
I shall come forth as gold.

There are many situations and circumstances in life occurring in the lives of people in all walks of life. Rich and poor alike experience the uncertainty of Cancer. Others unexpectedly experience the limitation of a stroke or heart attack. Those who were engaged in warfare experienced the suddenness of a life altered due to wounds sustained in military conflict. Who could predict or calculate an enemy's use of the IED (Improvised Explosive Device) and how devastating it would be? As a point of interest, Brookings Institute produced an article that indicated:

> While the IED is sometimes described as a new technology, it actually has a lengthy history. Ships

> loaded with explosives were used as far back as the 1500s, while various 'jury-rigged' bombs and mines were used in our own Civil War, such as at the naval battle of Mobile Bay and the land battle of Petersburg. Even the new(er) version of IEDs, who's explosively formed penetrators can pierce even the armor plating of the U.S. military's mine-resistant vehicles, actually dates back to World War II.
>
> The use of such weapons in the past was fairly limited and certainly without strategic consequences. The very name "improvised" was originally meant as a sort of putdown. An IED was used when you couldn't get something better, not something to be widely emulated. This turned with Iraq and Afghanistan, where the weapons helped neutralize the United States overwhelming advantage. They proved particularly effective against softer military targets such as Humvees, trucks and foot patrols, as well as civilians, and became the signature weapon in those wars. Last year in Afghanistan, they caused just over half of U.S. military deaths.

There are many areas in one's life that need to be brought under the authority of Jesus Christ. When I was young, our family lived in a ground floor tenement located across the street from the Black Eagle Bar. It was a place that had several patrons every day. Late at night, usually men who had over-imbibed, would stagger out of the Bad and try to walk to their destination. Some of them were loud and boisterous, while others wandered precariously. Some who have lived in a home where an alcoholic was part of the family, know first-hand the costs and peril of alcohol addiction. Finances that could benefit a family are misspent by the one who cannot contain or control his/her addiction. It reminds one of the significance in the words of wisdom, Proverbs 23:31-35 (NKJV),

> Do not look on the wine when it is red, When it sparkles in the cup, When it swirls around smoothly; At the last it bites like a serpent, And stings like a viper. Your eyes will see strange things, And your heart will utter perverse things. Yes, you will be like one who lies down in the midst of the sea, Or like one who lies at the top of the mast, saying: They have struck me, but I was not hurt; They have beaten me, but I did not feel it. When shall I awake, that I may seek another drink?

Addiction and Alcoholism are not always fully understood by the Church community. Prior to his death, my Father struggled with alcohol addiction. Intervention was not common in the early 1940s. One's family would rather ignore it or refer to the addiction as a sickness. There was a personal moment, early in my ministry, when a colleague who represented an agency of the denomination made the statement to me: "If I had known your Father was an alcoholic, I could've really loved you." Do you see and sense what is wrong with this man's statement? On the surface, it is an insensitive statement. It is obvious that all of what he was saying was both abstract and in the past tense. Love is never based on the "what" of one's life but on an individual's relationship and obedience to Jesus Christ who said, John 13:24-35,

> A new commandment I give to you, that you love one another; as I have loved you, that you also love one another. By this all will know that you are My disciples, if you have love for one another.

Do you see the difference between the agency representative's statement and the directive of Jesus Christ?

The agency representative was speaking in the past tense whereas Jesus Christ was speaking in the present and future tense. If only the words of Jesus Christ were remembered and practiced! If only Biblical Christians remembered to take a serious God seriously. Even though one may be the recipient of the wrong words being used by others, mercy, forgiveness, and the love of Jesus Christ must never be absent from one's thinking and implementation.

Individuals go through life with many valley-type experiences. They can weigh down upon a person and slow down enthusiasm for the spiritual tasks at hand. Three verses that should never be far from us are:

> Psalm 55:22, Cast your burden on the Lord, And He shall sustain you; He shall never permit the righteous to be moved.
>
> First Peter 5:6-7, Therefore humble yourselves under the mighty hand of God, that He may exalt you in due time, casting all your care upon Him, for He cares for you.
>
> Matthew 11:28-30, Come to Me, all you who labor and are heavy laden, and I will give you rest. Take My yoke upon you and learn from Me, for I am gentle and lowly in heart, and you will find rest for your souls. For My yoke is easy and My burden is light.

The words of the Joseph Scriven Hymn (1834-1916), asks in stanza three:

Are we weak and heavy-laden,
Cumbered with a load of care?
Precious Savior, still our refuge—
Take it to the Lord in prayer;
Do thy friends despise, forsake thee?
Take it to the Lord in prayer;
In His arms He'll take and shield thee,
Thou wilt find a solace there.

May these words uplift your carking (burdensome) anxieties and cause you to "Rejoice in the Lord" today and all the days of your life. May this be your identification and witness for the Lord Jesus Christ.

16. Authenticity

> One day as Jesus was walking along the shore of the Sea of Galilee, he saw two brothers, Simon, also called Peter, and Andrew, throwing a net into the water, for they fished for a living. Jesus called out to them: Come, follow me, and I will show you how to fish for people! And they left their nets at once and followed him. A little farther up the shore he saw two other brothers, James and John, sitting in a boat with their father, Zebedee, repairing their nets. And he called them to come, too. They immediately followed him, leaving the boat and their father behind.
>
> Matthew 4:18-22 (NLT)

In Matthew 4, Jesus had been fasting for forty days and nights. During that time, the devil subjected Him to various temptations in the areas of personal lust: the eye, the flesh and pride. First John 2:15-17 (NLT) lists these same areas of temptation for every believer. They are specified in verse 16, "The world offers only a craving for physical pleasure, a craving for everything we see, and pride in our achievements and possessions. These are not from the Father but are from this world." The NKJV translation is: "For all that *is* in the world—the lust of the flesh, the lust of the eyes, and the pride of life—is not of the Father but is of the world."

When Jesus calls His disciples, He chooses men from different backgrounds, experiences and education. To all who are called, He uses the statement: "Follow Me, and I will make you…" He will make them into the men He wants them to be. They will be trained and enabled so they can minister for Him in a variety of situations and among a cross-section of people.

After the disciples have been chosen and their learning from Jesus has begun, there is a phrase given that deserves one's attention. In Mark 3:14, "Jesus appointed twelve that they might be with him and that he might send them out to preach." The phrase to note is: "that they might be with Him." Anything else they would be called to do or be pales in comparison with the vital and purposeful relationship of being "with Him." There is a Hymn written by Mary D. James (1871), All For Jesus, that contains words that typify the need and importance of being "with Him." The learning and making experience will result in a fixation upon Jesus and His will.

Let my hands perform His bidding,
Let my feet run in His ways;
Let my eyes see Jesus only,
Let my lips speak forth His praise.

Since my eyes were fixed on Jesus,
I've lost sight of all beside;
So enchained my spirit's vision,
Looking at the Crucified.

When Jesus chose the twelve to follow Him and to be with Him, they had no idea where this would lead them or what they would become. Their learning was a process of learning. The more they were fixated on Jesus and His will for them the sooner they would be more fully equipped for the task He had planned for them. For instance, they probably had no thought about becoming an Apostle who would represent and serve Jesus Christ after His departure. A basic requirement of being "with Him" is to observe how he ministered and to whom He would reach out and heal. They would one day be called upon as eye-witnesses of all that He said and did. They would also learn how to preach effectively and where, when and how miracles would become part of what they would do in Jesus' name.

Would they sometimes try to be and do ministry before they were able to do so? Yes! Would they have moments and situations in which they would fail? Yes! Would there be times when they would stray from the foundational principles they were being taught? Yes! Would they ever have negative thoughts and expressions about Jesus? Yes! Most of the time, Jesus would address them with the question: "Why is it you have so little faith?" Jesus would also use the question: "Why is it that you have no faith?" How often do we find ourselves in similar situations comparable to those of His disciples? How often is it because of the question Jesus posed to His disciples about little faith and no faith?

In the larger picture, Jesus wanted His disciples to be totally authentic. They were to represent who He was and how He lived. The comparison was always with the Scribes, Pharisees and Sadducees. Jesus pointed out that they were known for their pretense and blatant hypocrisy. In Matthew 23, Jesus pronounces a series of woes against the Scribes and Pharisees. He notes they were zealous but with an incorrect emphasis and purpose. They knew the Law of Moses and added their interpretations and applications to it. In Matthew 23:28, Jesus defines and condemn them: "You outwardly appear righteous to others, but within you are full of hypocrisy and lawlessness." Earlier, Jesus said of the Scribes and Pharisees: "Woe to you, scribes and Pharisees, hypocrites! For you travel across sea and land to make a single proselyte, and when he becomes a proselyte, you make him twice as much a child of hell (Greek Word Gehenna) as yourselves." In Matthew 28:33, Jesus pronounces: "You serpents, you brood of vipers, how are you to escape being sentenced to hell?"

Would the disciples succumb to the persuasiveness and coercions of the Scribes and Pharisees? Would they consider any advantage to being part of the societal and religious devotees of their day? Would they let their sense of self-sufficiency supersede their commitment to Goddependency? Even though they heard the woes pronounced by Jesus against the Scribes and Pharisees, would they make a choice to be identified with the accepted societal and religious culture of their day? Would this be a time where their choice would be to count everything loss in order to know Jesus Christ and be completely identified with Him. If you lived in that day, what would your choice have been? If you fast forward to the present day, what choices have you made that define who you are within the societal and religious culture today? What distinguishing spiritual characteristics and qualities are obvious in your life?

Some of the distinguishing marks of the Biblical Christian include an adherence and application of the chief end of man. It is to glorify God and enjoy Him forever. Our lives should radiate and echo the glory of His presence, Jesus clearly stated this necessity in John 13:31-32, "Now the Son of Man is glorified, and God is glorified in Him. If God is glorified in Him, God will also glorify the Son in Himself and will glorify Him at once." On a personal level, the contemporary worship song written by Ron Kenoly should be the song of our hearts and lives:

Oh, the glory of Your presence;
We Your temple, Give You reverence.
Come and rise from Your rest
And be blessed by our praise;
As we glory in Your embrace;
As Your presence Now fills this place.

It is a necessary and unique privilege to glorify Jesus Christ in our lives and all of our thoughts, words and deeds.

Based upon John 13:34-35, there must also be an unfailing spirit of camaraderie and love for the people of God. Jesus stated: "Love one another. As I have loved you, so also you must love one another. By this all men will know that you are My disciples, if you love one another." In other words,

Jesus is teaching that true discipleship is not just talk but it must be demonstrated by one's walk. John would later write, First John 1:5-7,

> And this is the message we have heard from Him and announce to you: God is light, and in Him there is no darkness at all. If we say we have fellowship with Him yet walk in the darkness, we lie and do not practice the truth. But if we walk in the light as He is in the light, we have fellowship with one another, and the blood of Jesus His Son cleanses us from all sin.

This is a basic requirement for every Biblical Christian, "to walk in the light as He is in the light." It dovetails with John 1:7-8, "He (John) came as a witness to testify about the Light, so that through him everyone might believe. He himself was not the Light, but he came to testify about the Light." The objective for the one who walks in the light as stated in Matthew 5:16, "In the same way, let your light shine before men, that they may see your good deeds and glorify your Father in heaven." Does your light shine among people in your community and sphere of contacts? Do the glorify your Father in heaven because of how you consistently live among them? Do you remember that it is not by talk but by your walk you will have the greatest influence for Jesus Christ? People have become cynical and are longing for authenticity. Does your life demonstrate that you have been unchained and become free indeed in Jesus Christ? This is the authenticity people need and are craving.

Dr. A. W. Tozer said:

> We are not to look like or act like other people; rather, we are to look like Jesus Christ. We are to act like Christ. We are to do the things Christ would do in the power and demonstration of the Holy Spirit.

As Jesus was approaching the Cross, Hos disciples avowed their complete loyalty to Him. They even indicated they were ready to die for Him and with Him. Matthew 26:35, Peter emphatically stated: "Even if I must die with You, I will never deny You." In like manner, the remainder of the disciples (minus Judas Iscariot) concurred with Peter's words: "And the rest of the disciples said the same." How quickly this assertion of loyalty would change. When the mob was at its most violent, the disciples had withdrawn. It quickly resulted in their fleeing for their own safety, Matthew 26:56 indicates, "Then all the disciples deserted Him and fled." Jesus was alone as He suffered, bled and died. Benjamin H. Price wrote the words:

It was alone the Savior prayed
In dark Gethsemane;
Alone He drained the bitter cup
And suffered there for me.

Refrain:

Alone, alone, He bore it all alone;
He gave Himself to save His own,
He suffered, bled and died alone, alone.

Throughout Church History, followers of Jesus Christ have been subjected to persecution and martyrdom. In data released in 2015, we have the following estimates of martyrdom in our world:

> A new article series in Christian History magazine says a global war is being waged against Christians. The reports are in the latest edition of the quarterly publication and co-authored by members of Voice of the Martyrs USA.
>
> Although they particularly examined the persecution of Christians in the last 300 years, they also contain figures going back through Christian history.

> The data, attributed to the late researcher David B Barrett, puts the number of Christians martyred since the time of Jesus at 70 million.
>
> It puts the number of Christians systematically exterminated in Nazi Germany at a million, while the number of Orthodox Christians and others murdered in Russia between 1917 and 1950 at 15 million.

The listing and numbers could be extended to include places like China and India where Christianity is forbidden. We tend to be unaware that restrictions in the United States of America have been imposed against Christianity. Prayer and Bible Reading being removed from the Public Schools (1962-1963) was the start of the nation being on the road of secularism. The law regarding abortion accelerated cultural decline and a general acceptance of the law. As we near more than sixty-million abortions since the law was passed in 1973, it seems to go unnoticed in the contemporary culture. More recently, we have been told that "Merry Christmas" should be changed to "Happy Holidays." There was very little vocal opposition to that recommendation. The same was true when the Creche (Nativity Scene) was disallowed in public places. Traditional Christmas Carols are replaced by popular Christmas songs, and it is generally accepted. All of this, and several other things, has moved the nation closer to the slippery slope of cultural demise. The Church has been more silent than vocal with the changes that are taking place.

Are we allowing the nation and culture to become chained and shackled by the preferences of the more bold and vocal? Is anyone willing to stand in the gap and issue warning to the nation about its drift to being unrighteous and lacking godliness? What has happened to the display and vocalization of John 3:16 (the Gospel)? What has happened to the Biblical Church and Christian being authentic and representing the

True Light – Jesus Christ – in a world of decadence and chaos?

We should never make the choice of the disciples, who at the crucial hour being faced by Jesus Christ, fled in fear. Jesus wanted then, as He does now, for His Bride, the Church, and His people to be authentic by sharing with all that they can be unchained and unshackled in Jesus Christ and realize being free indeed. May our commitment be:

I have decided to follow Jesus;
No turning back, no turning back.

The world behind me, the cross before me;
No turning back, no turning back.

Though none go with me, still I will follow;
No turning back, no turning back.

My cross I'll carry, till I see Jesus;
No turning back, no turning back.

Will you decide now to follow Jesus?
No turning back, no turning back.

17. Cautionary Words

Moreover, brethren, I do not want you to be unaware that all our fathers were under the cloud, all passed through the sea, all were baptized into Moses in the cloud and in the sea, all ate the same spiritual food, and all drank the same spiritual drink. For they drank of that spiritual Rock that followed them, and that Rock was Christ. But with most of them God was not well pleased, for their bodies were scattered in the wilderness. Now these things became our examples, to the intent that we should not lust after evil things as they also lusted.

First Corinthians 10:1-6 (Selected – NKJV)

A common phrase in the English language is: "throw caution to the wind." The Cambridge Dictionary entry states the general meaning is: "doing things without fear or proper thought." Some of the synonyms are: daredevil, foolhardy, impetuous, impulsive, reckless, trigger-happy. The Urban Dictionary entry is: "to disregard any risk or potential disaster when undertaking any enterprise or venture." When we reflect upon our culture, there are evidences that within government, as well as societal values, caution has been thrown to the wind. The foundation principles stated in the Constitution of the United States are being disregarded and core values of the nation challenged. In recent times, we have seen efforts to revisit and re-write history. The moral values of the founding fathers are brought into question. The basis of the Civil War are being re-interpreted. Symbols from the historical past are being removed or destroyed. In effect, history is being sacrificed and a new narrative is being embraced.

The religious culture has been re-examining its core values and foundational principles. Biblical doctrines have been scrutinized and Biblical instruction blatantly defied. The value of life was reinterpreted and altered when abortion was legalized. God's statements about homosexuality, lesbianism, transgender preferences, Sodom and Gomorrah, etc. are systematically dismantled by the Church, as well as the government. The Church should ask itself whether or not the culture is impacting the Church rather than the Church impacting the culture. A valid question that needs to be revisited and answered is: What happened to men of God standing on and for the Word of God in the twenty-first century? What is the rational for embracing teaching contrary to that stated by God and recorded in Holy Scripture? What answer will one give to Almighty God on the day of judgment when the question will be asked by Him: Why did you ignore My Word and defy My standards?

It might do one well to remember the words in First Corinthians 10:12, "Therefore let him who thinks he stands take heed lest he fall." The reminder of this possibility of falling was rehearsed on the second day of Passover in the Jewish tradition. Psalm 106 was read and followed by the reciting of Psalm 126. The general structure of Psalm 106 indicates the following:

Verses 1 through 5 are words that ae filled with praise to and worship of the Lord. The ones who can offer such praise and worship are identified:

> *Who can utter the mighty acts of the Lord? Who can declare all His praise? Blessed are those who keep justice, and he who does righteousness at all times!*

Verses 6 and 7 are words of confession. Reference is made to their historical reality bondage in Egypt and rebellion at the Red Sea. The confession is clear and to the point:

> *We have sinned with our fathers. We have committed iniquity. We have done wickedly.*

Verses 8 through 12 begins with "nevertheless" (other translations and the New Testament state it as "But God"). Despite their deliberate rebellion, God reached out to them in His mercy and compassion.

> *Nevertheless He saved them for His name's sake, that He might make His mighty power known…He saved them from the hand of him who hated them, and redeemed them from the hand of the enemy.*

Verses 13 through 15 represents how quickly people forget the goodness and grace of the Lord and return to carnal behavior.

> *They soon forgot His works; they did not wait for His counsel, But lusted exceedingly in the wilderness, and tested God in the desert. He gave them their request but sent leanness into their soul.*

Verses 16 through 43 indicates the numerous actions of the people in their disregard of God, His mercy, His protection, His provision and His standards. Verses 24-25 is the core issue that resulted in God's indictment, their exile and bondage once again:

> *Then they despised the pleasant land; they did not believe His word, but complained in their tents, and did not heed the voice of the Lord.*

Verses 44 through 46 underscores that God's compassion and mercy are always available and ready to be shown. The people have been enslaved and have known the difficulties of bondage once again. They are miserable and agonizing in their circumstances. God's heart is touched. There is another "nevertheless" (But God) that includes His basis for acting in their behalf, "according to the multitude of His mercies":

> *Nevertheless He regarded their affliction, when He heard their cry; and for their sake He remembered His*

> *covenant and relented according to the multitude of His mercies. He also made them to be pitied by all those who carried them away captive.*

Verses 47 and 48 are a benediction:

> *Save us, O Lord our God, and gather us from among the Gentiles, to give thanks to Your holy name, to triumph in Your praise. Blessed be the Lord God of Israel from everlasting to everlasting! And let all the people say, "Amen!" Praise the Lord!*

Psalm 126 reviews and rehearses the people's joyful return to Zion. They have been brought back by the power and grace of the Lord. They return with laughter and singing. Their bondage had been ended and once again they were free indeed. The word of verse 3 express the reason for joy, singing and laughter: "The Lord has done great things for us, and we are glad."

Despite the darkness and bleakness of the culture in any period of history, the questions that need to be asked and answered are several. Can any one individual or spiritually committed persons influence or impact the culture? Does one's life have any value as illumination in the midst of darkness? Can you and/or I make a positive difference amid the considerable number of culturally negative trends and customs? Glenn Sunshine writing on the subject of the culture wrote:

> *One of the signs of a great society is the diligence with which it passes culture from one generation to the next. This culture is the embodiment of everything the people of that society hold dear: its religious faith, it's heroes...when one generation no longer esteems its own heritage and fails to pass the torch to its children, it is saying in essence that the very foundational principles and experiences that make the society what*

it is are no longer valid. This leaves that generation without any sense of definition or direction.
Winston Churchill from "Never Give In", Page 190.

What heritage, legacy and cultural values are we passing on to our generation? Our children's generation? Our Grandchildren's generation? What will they remember about us and the things we cherished the most? What memories will they have to pass on to their children? The dedication of this book will include the words of Psalm 127:3, "children are a heritage from the Lord" and Psalm 128:3, "Your children like olive plants all around your table." At some point, all of us have sung the children's hymn, Jesus Loves Me. One line uses the words: "Little ones to Him belong, they are weak but He is strong." This was very obvious as this chapter was being written. Word was received that our great Grandson, Keaton, who had been treated for leukemia from two and one-half years of age, entered into eternity on May 10, 2018 at eight years of age. This precious little boy leaves a heritage of having been a great example for all who knew him. He was strong and joyful despite his pain and physical malady. He loved and cared for his younger brothers. He had a sharp mind, a tender heart and was a positive influence for all who knew him.

His Dad wrote the following words to and about his son, Keaton. The words flow from a grateful and sorrowing heart:

My dear sweet Keaton,
Thank you for showing me what it means to be truly selfless. Your love and compassion for others along with the positivity and joy you lived your life, in the face of everything you had to go through, was absolutely amazing to witness. The cross you had to bear for the majority of your life was, quite simply, unfair. Yet you carried it with such grace and strength,

never complaining and continued to move forward. You surpassed anything and everything I could have imagined in a son, and I am eternally grateful that God chose your mother and me to be your parents. I am infinitely proud of you, Keaton. I have loved you since before you were born and will love you for the rest of my life. Thank you for letting me be your Daddy.
Enjoy Heaven, my beautiful boy. I love you! Dad.

What heritage, legacy, influence and values will all who know you think about when you are no longer physically present in this world and culture? What will your children, grandchildren, great-grandchildren want to know and emulate based upon your life? The words and music written by John Mohr (1988) and sung by Steve Green summarize the importance of our heritage and legacy for those who come behind us.

Oh may all who come behind us find us faithful,
May the fire of our devotion light their way,
May the footprints that we leave
Lead them to believe,
And the lives we live inspire them to obey,
Oh may all who come behind us find us faithful.

A Facebook post by Karen Franz regarding death and grief was shared by Steve Sellers. It is titled: "*When Grief Turns To Joy*." Some excerpts from that post are:

Very truly I tell you, you will weep and mourn while the world rejoices. You will grieve, but your grief will turn to joy. So with you: Now is your time of grief, but I will see you again and you will rejoice, and no one will take away your joy (John 16:20, 22).

These are the words of Jesus to his disciples, concerning his death and resurrection. He tells them that he will be leaving them...While he's dead and in the grave, they will weep and mourn, but the world will rejoice, because of their hate for him. He tells them they will grieve, but their grief will turn to joy. He says: Now is your time of grief, but I will see you again, (speaking of his resurrection), and you will rejoice, and no one will take away your joy...Just like the disciples, we are living in times, which bring us much grief, because of the negativity and hostility towards our Christian values. The true believer knows that because of the death of Jesus Christ, the overcomer of this sinful world, has brought the greatest gift, ever given to mankind, the gift of forgiveness of sins, and an eternal home in heaven.

This reminded me of the words to the Hymn that states the reality of the resurrection of Jesus Christ and what it means for all Biblical Christians. With the death of our eight-year-old Great Grandson, and applying some of these words to his six-year struggle with Leukemia, the following words filled my thoughts and resulted in joy that replaced sorrow:

The strife is o'er, the battle done;
The victory of life is won;
The song of triumph has begun:
Alleluia!

The powers of death have done their worst;
But Christ their legions has dispersed;
Let shouts of holy joy outburst:
Alleluia!

Lord, by the stripes which wounded You,
In us You've won the victory too,
That we may live, and sing to You:
Alleluia!

The chapter title is about Cautionary Words. It is so easy for a person to become bogged down in life and despair because of the reach of our culture. What hope can one have in this life? When the best we can do seems to be wrong, and success in life appears to be out of one's reach, how can one find relief and escape from the mundane and that which so easily enslaves one to its dictates? The words of First Corinthians 10:13 (NKJV) should be an encouragement as they are read, believed and applied:

> *No temptation has overtaken you except such as is common to man; but God is faithful, who will not allow you to be tempted beyond what you are able, but with the temptation will also make the way of escape, that you may be able to bear it.*

Your source of being unchained is Jesus Christ. In Luke 4:18-19, Jesus is in the synagogue and opened the scroll of Isaiah the prophet. He read and applied the prophet's words as His purpose, mission, and focus:

> *The Spirit of the Lord is upon Me, because He has anointed Me to preach the gospel to the poor; He has sent Me to heal the brokenhearted; to proclaim liberty to the captives and recovery of sight to the blind, to set at liberty those who are oppressed; to proclaim the acceptable year of the Lord.*

If you are brokenhearted, Jesus Christ can and will break those chains and grant you His freedom. If you are a captive of some habit or addiction, Jesus Christ can and will break those chains that bind you and set you free indeed. Have you come to Him? Do you know Him? Do you know the full ramification of being free indeed? Jesus Christ is ready, willing and able to embrace you into His free indeed family!

18. My Portion

> Yet I am always with you; you hold me by my right hand. You guide me with your counsel, and afterward you will take me into glory. Whom have I in heaven but you? And earth has nothing I desire besides you. My flesh and my heart may fail, but God is the strength of my heart and my portion forever.
>
> Psalm 73:23-26

From a secular point of view, portion is a word with a wide-variety of meaning. It is probably used most often in terms of food preparation and the type and amount of food that is well-balanced and adequate for one's physical need and good health. That specification is referred to as a portion. In general it means: (1) a part of any whole; (2) an amount of food served for one person; a serving or helping. It can also mean: (3) the part of any estate that goes to an heir or a next of kin; (4) a dowry or an inheritance; (5) to divide into or distribute in portions or equal shares.

From a spiritual point of view, the idea of a portion has a different application. To illustrate, Psalm 73 begins with a very negative perspective of the world, culture and life in general. It would be easy for one to join ranks with Asaph (the writer of the Psalm) and conclude that life means nothing more than difficulty, discouragement and misery. Things for the godly always seem to be moving from bad to worse. Those deemed to be evil seem to move from success to success, whereas the righteous struggle with never having a sense of achievement because of one being overwhelmed with the challenges of life. Rather than success, there are failures. Rather than adequacy, there are limitless difficulties. If only the spiritually minded knew some of the ease of the secular culture.

It would be ideal if one lived in a juxtaposition world and would mentally turn Psalm 73 around to Psalm 37 and join ranks with David (the writer of the Psalm 37), then the perspective might also be changed from a negative to a positive perspective. Psalm 37 begins with a two-word statement: “Fret not!” and quickly focuses upon the Lord and the need to trust Him, to commit one’s way to Him and to find one’s delight in Him.

This contrast and transition is brought to mind in the words written by Civilia D. Martin (1905), His Eye Is On The Sparrow. Some of the lyric includes:

Why should I feel discouraged?
Why should the shadows come?
Why should my heart be lonely,
and long for heaven and home?
When Jesus is my portion -
My constant friend is He:
His eye is on the sparrow,
and I know He watches me.

Whenever I am tempted,
whenever clouds arise,
When songs give place to sighing,
when hope within me dies,
I draw the closer to Him,
from care He sets me free;
His eye is on the sparrow,
and I know He watches me.

When thinking about the contrast drawn in Psalm 73, there was an illustration used by a Bible Professor that addressed how easily one can lose perspective and begin to falter with doubts and fears rather than being fully focused and moving forward with confidence, faith and hope. He used a pair of Trifocal Glasses. His comment was the difficulty one has when adjusting his/her vision to adapt to the new lenses. He said the problem comes from looking at the trifocal lens itself and attempting to physically decide where to focus one's eyes. The remedy is to look at the object before one rather than struggling with adjusting to the trifocal lens. What is the spiritual application? It means there is a need to apply Hebrews 12:2, Looking to Jesus, the object of our faith, rather than the details of life that would distract us from seeing Him, the author and completer of our faith.

In what ways is Jesus the adequate portion one needs for daily living? What do I know about Him that assures me of His vigilance and care?

Psalm 23 and John 10 – He is my Shepherd.
Psalm 91 – He is my Refuge and Fortress
Psalm 32 – He is my Hiding Place
Psalm 28 – He is my Strength and Shield
Psalm 18 – He is my Defender
Psalm 118 – He is my Song
II Thessalonians 3 – He is my Protector
Psalm 34 – He is my Deliverer
Romans 15 – He is my Encourager
Isaiah 41 and 43 – He is my Redeemer
I John 2 – He is my Advocate
Psalm 73 – He is my Portions.

To add to this list, your self-study should take you to the Gospel of John and the seven "I AM" statements Jesus made about Himself.

John 6:35 – I AM the bread of life.
John 8:12 – I AM the light of the world.
John 10:9 – I AM the door.
John 10:11 – I AM the good shepherd.
John 11:25 – I AM then resurrection and the life.
John 14:6 – I AM the way, the truth, and the life.

John 15:1 – I AM the true vine.
Revelation 22:13 – I AM the alpha and omega.
The references above are representative of the many things that Jesus Christ was made to be and has become for His followers. A worship song written by Charles Price Jones summarizes:

Jesus Christ is made to me,
All I need, all I need,
He alone is all my plea, He is all I need.
Refrain
Wisdom righteousness and power,
Holiness forevermore,
My redemption full and sure,
He is all I need.

Jesus is my all in all,
All I need, all I need,
While He keeps I cannot fall, He is all I need.

He redeemed me when He died,
All I need, all I need,
I with Him was crucified, He is all I need.

Glory, glory to the Lamb,
All I need, all I need,
By His Spirit sealed I am, He is all I need.

Having knowledge of who Jesus Christ is and what He claimed to be is fine. Having a personal relationship with and living in the presence of Jesus Christ is that which makes a significant difference in and for one's life. The question one must answer is: Do I have only a knowledge about who Jesus Christ is, or do I know Him personally, and intimately because I have committed my life to Him? A Hymn that contains an interesting refrain, In The Garden (C. Austin Miles, 1912), addresses what it means to know Jesus Christ intimately and personally:

And He walks with me, and He talks with me,
And He tells me I am His own;
And the joy we share as we tarry there,
None other has ever known.

This is the relationship Adam and Eve knew in the Garden of Eden before they yielded to temptation and disobeyed God. At their moment of greatest failure, God was gracious toward them as He sought them out and clothed them. It was after His compassionate acts that they both were driven out of the Garden. It necessitated an entirely different way and means to have fellowship with the Almighty God. They would now have to sacrifice a lamb to atone for their sins. They would have to learn the standards of God and the necessary discipline to follow them as closely as possible. It will be in the new relationship they will learn that God is their portion and all they need.

The chapter began with reference to Psalm 73. The focus of Asaph is summarized in verses 2-3, "My steps had nearly slipped. For I *was* envious of the boastful, When I saw the prosperity of the wicked." This is always a danger if the Biblical Christian compares Biblical values with those of the secular culture. The viewpoint of Asaph is common and understandable to a degree, especially when he wrote (Verse 7): "Their eyes bulge with abundance; They have more than heart could wish." He viewed all of this as being grossly unfair. It would be easy to be sympathetic to his feelings and expression of them.

What is the remedy for the Biblical Christian in the twenty-first century? There is an expression – "the more things change the more similar they are. Asaph wrote his words approximately three-thousand years ago. Our contemporary culture and world represents much of what

Psalm 73 is expressing. Life does not seem fair. The rich seem to become richer while the average person remains static. At first blush, it also seems unfair. It's as though Asaph can no longer contain himself and he writes in verses 11-14:

> And they say: How does God know? And is there knowledge in the Most High? Behold, these are the ungodly, who are always at ease; they increase in riches. Surely, I have cleansed my heart in vain, and washed my hands in innocence. For all day long, I have been plagued and chastened every morning.

His resolve occurs in Verses 16-17,

> When I thought how to understand this, it was too painful for me, Until I went into the sanctuary of God; Then I understood their end.

We should take special note of the sanctuary of God. The sanctuary represented the presence of God in the midst of His people. The furnishings of the sanctuary also provided reminders of the constancy of the Lord's care for His people through all generations. Asaph's resolve and perspective are changed as he focuses upon the reality of God. Verses 25-28 indicate this change. Asaph wrote:

> Whom have I in heaven but You? and there is none upon earth that I desire besides You. My flesh and my heart fail; But God is the strength of my heart and my portion forever. For indeed, those who are far from You shall perish; You have destroyed all those who desert You for harlotry. But it is good for me to draw near to God; I have put my trust in the Lord God, that I may declare all Your works.

One of the reasons for God's people assembling each week in the Church is intended to serve to the same end. It is a time to recall the faithfulness and goodness of God. It enables God's people to gain God's perspective for His people. Hebrews 10:21-25 shares God's purpose for His people as they continue to seek and worship Him in the culture of the day:

> Having a High Priest over the house of God, let us draw near with a true heart in full assurance of faith, having our hearts sprinkled from an evil conscience and our bodies washed with pure water. Let us hold fast the confession of our hope without wavering, for He who promised is faithful. And let us consider one another in order to stir up love and good works, not forsaking the assembling of ourselves together, as is the manner of some, but exhorting one another, and so much the more as you see the Day approaching.

The purpose in coming to the Sanctuary is to gain a greater insight in terms of who God is and what God does. It is a place of refuge from the demands and lifestyle of the contemporary culture. It is a place where the child of God knows the full benefit of being unchained, set loose, and knowing the liberty and freedom that is available in Christ alone. Edith Margaret Clarkson (1915-2008) wrote the Hymn, We Come, O Christ, To Thee. The first stanza states the special relationship one has in relationship to Jesus Christ. This should also be the result and benefit of having come together in the sanctuary of God with the people of God. It provides us with the correct perspective and clear focus regarding who we are in Jesus Christ.

We come, O Christ, to Thee,
True Son of God and man,
By whom all things consist,
In whom all life began:
In Thee alone we live and move
And have our being in Thy love.

May you continue to walk in the liberty in which Jesus Christ has set you free – unchained and free indeed.

19. My Vision

> Multitudes, multitudes, in the valley of decision! For the day of the Lord is near in the valley of decision.
>
> Joel 3:14 (ESV)
>
> Where there is no vision, the people perish: but he that keeps the law, happy is he.
>
> Proverbs 29:18 (KJV)

It is basic and important to know both the heart and mind of Jesus Christ for His world and His people. There is a clear distinction drawn between those who share the Lord's vision for His sheep and those who do not. It reveals whether or not one approaches God's flock as a mercenary (working or acting merely for money or some other reward), as compared with one who serves regardless of any monetary or tangible gain. Jesus Christ made a clear statement in this matter, John 10:11-15 (ESV), when He said:

> I am the good shepherd. The good shepherd lays down his life for the sheep. He who is a hired hand and not a shepherd, who does not own the sheep, sees the wolf coming and leaves the sheep and flees, and the wolf snatches them and scatters them. He flees because he is a hired hand and cares nothing for the sheep. I am the good shepherd. I know my own and my own know me, just as the Father knows me and I know the Father; and I lay down my life for the sheep.

What does the Good Shepherd want us to learn from Him about shepherding? How does He want us to function in and with His flock? Some lessons we learn include His use of three parables in Luke 15 – The Lost Sheep; The Lost Coin; and The Lost Son. The emphasis in Luke 15:3-7, The Lost

Sheep is on the caring and concerned shepherd who seeks for the one lost sheep. He rescues it from the place of its lostness, places it on his shoulders and returns it to the fold. In doing so, the shepherd rejoices with others because the one sheep who was lost has been found. The parable relates it to the Gospel and the lost soul who is sought and found. Jesus summarized (verse 7): "there will be more joy in heaven over one sinner who repents than over ninety-nine righteous persons who need no repentance."

The Good Shepherd wants shepherds who are willing to face any opposition and to be engaged in any dangerous circumstance for the sake of His flock. The powerful illustration is when David met with King Saul and volunteered to face the enemy of God's people. Goliath was a cause of fear and trembling among the people. King Saul was hesitant to allow David to face such a formidable opponent. David made a bold and confident statement to King Saul, First Samuel 17:34-36,

> But David said to Saul: Your servant used to keep sheep for his father. And when there came a lion, or a bear, and took a lamb from the flock, I went after him and struck him and delivered it out of his mouth. And if he arose against me, I caught him by his beard and struck him and killed him. Your servant has struck down both lions and bears, and this uncircumcised Philistine shall be like one of them, for he has defied the armies of the living God.

The Good Shepherd wants the care of His sheep to be on a continuum rather than occasional. Peter underscored this when he wrote, First Peter 5:2-4,

> Shepherd the flock of God that is among you, exercising oversight, not under compulsion, but willingly, as God would have you; not for shameful gain, but eagerly; not domineering over those in your

> charge, but being examples to the flock. And when the chief Shepherd appears, you will receive the unfading crown of glory.

The commitment of David and the instruction of Peter serve a common purpose. One must emulate The Good Shepherd among His sheep at all times and in all situations. There will be times when such care will be aid times of distress or conflict. It may even have elements of danger. In the situation of spousal and/or child abuse, it may require rescue. In church related shepherding, the Pastor may be in the forefront of dangerous situations.

It serves us well to know the origin of the term – Pastor. It is a Latin expression meaning to shepherd; to be a feeder; to put to pasture. Overall, the Pastor is one who leads as well as feeds God's flock. The Pastor is vigilant and ready to face any challenge as he carries out his duties to protect God's flock from predators and danger. He is to feed the flock with that which provides the greatest and healthiest nourishment.

The hireling is matter-of-fact in what he does with the sheep. He is focused on his monetary return rather than the well-being of the flock. The hireling is unwilling to risk his own well-being for that of the flock. If a "lion or bear" is nearby, unlike David, the hireling will flee to protect his own life. In doing so, he leaves the flock to become prey for that which will ravage them. The hireling is absent of mercy and grace in terms of the flock. In that sense, he is very similar to the mercenary who will join an army for monetary reward rather than protecting the particular government the army should be defending. It would not be unusual for a mercenary soldier to flee from conflict. Being AWOL (absent without leave) is of no great concern for him. Personal survival is paramount. The hireling and the mercenary are very similar.

On the website, The Mercenary Trader, the posted motto is: A Community Of Ruthless Profiteers. Their Mercenary Creed is also posted (and explained):

> Thou shalt heed the price action; thou shalt respect the risk; Monitor thy equity curve; Thou shalt go for the jugular; Thou shalt focus on making money; Thou shalt go short as well as long; To thine own self be true.

Regarding the second creedal statement (Thou shalt respect the risk!), there is a statement of purpose given:

> When I was a child, I traded as a child, not giving proper respect to risk. But now I am a Mercenary, and so now I trade like a Mercenary, giving risk its proper due. My trading capital is my life force; like an aviator's fuel or an ocean diver's air supply, I shall monitor it with passion and precision. I shall survive for only then can I thrive; as Sun Tzu instructed, I shall wait by the side of the river for the bodies of my enemies to float by. In respecting the risk, I shall continue on as my enemy falters…and in surviving, my opportunities shall multiply.

In this creedal statement, there are no indicators of either mercy of grace. The Mercenary is merciless. The mercenary creedal statement is a different attitude and purpose than that shared in Second Corinthians 8:1-5 (NIV) by a typical Biblical flock of God,

> We want you to know about the grace that God has given the Macedonian churches. Out of the most severe trial, their overflowing joy and their extreme poverty welled up in rich generosity. For I testify that they gave as much as they were able, and even beyond their ability. Entirely on their own, they urgently pleaded with us for the privilege of sharing in this service to the saints. And they did not do as we

> expected, but they gave themselves first to the Lord and then to us in keeping with God's will.

At this moment in time in our world and culture, it appears that the days immediately ahead are trending toward being more bleak than bright. More dangerous situations loom on the horizon. Greater risks may have to be taken. The flock of God is under greater attack. It reminds one of that which Paul wrote, Second Timothy 3:1-5,

> But mark this: There will be terrible times in the last days. People will be lovers of themselves, lovers of money, boastful, proud, abusive, disobedient to their parents, ungrateful, unholy, without love, unforgiving, slanderous, without self-control, brutal, not lovers of the good, treacherous, rash, conceited, lovers of pleasure rather than lovers of God - having a form of godliness but denying its power. Have nothing to do with such people.

Have we arrived at this point? Do Paul's words describe what the world, culture and church is becoming or has become? In some churches, there are too many who fall into the category of mercenary or hireling than that of a Pastor who cares and who is willing to sacrifice everything - including his own life – for the sake of the flock. Our culture has grown more accustomed to things and personal possessions or assets. For us, it may mean greater difficulty to adjust to less. What will the church do and become? Will its vision be the same as the vision of The Good Shepherd? Will the Biblical Church and Biblical Christian function under the free indeed (John 8:36) banner of the Lord Jesus Christ? Will we know the full ramification of living and being unchained?

We must consider whether or not our perspective as a people of God has become too myopic. Rather than a broad perspective, we have adapted to a narrow focus. Many nations in our world have coped with less and dealt with considerable hardship. It is sad to see how far American Churches have drifted from the Macedonian mentality and commitment to a higher purpose and a greater good. How many churches are living by the model of Second Corinthians 8? As part of your thinking, consider the size of the Church Buildings and Complexes that have become part of the religious scene of our times, and the "bragging rights" that seem to come from what has been built? Were the buildings erected to the Glory of God alone, or subtly, to the praise that comes to man/men? Was this done on the basis of The Mercenary Creed or on a commitment to The Beatitudes?

Along with a mercenary mentality, being merciless is also a growing tendency. The Church is being operated more as a business than a place of ministering to the spiritual status and needs of people. Those who are committed to the vision and purpose of the Lord Jesus Christ find some basic questions relevant to what the Church is becoming. The basic questions would include: Do you ever have a sense that no matter what you attempt to do you seem to be on the losing side? Do you ever feel that you are part of a cruel culture that seems to be headed on a crash course with history and destiny? Do you ever think that no matter how generous you are and regardless of the good you attempt to do (and want to do) that reciprocally - you rarely experience similar treatment or consideration? Do you feel or conclude we are living in a "dog-eat-dog" world where the sense of equity, fairness, kindness, mercy, grace and generosity are diminishing rapidly?

If only we could return, know and be engaged in the reality of Stanza 3 in The Church's One Foundation:

'Mid toil and tribulation,
And tumult of her war,
She waits the consummation

Of peace for evermore;
Till, with the vision glorious,
Her longing eyes are blest,
And the great Church victorious
Shall be the Church at rest.

20. My Desire

> In this the love of God was manifested toward us, that God has sent His only begotten Son into the world, that we might live through Him. In this is love, not that we loved God, but that He loved us and sent His Son to be the propitiation for our sins. Beloved, if God so loved us, we also ought to love one another.
>
> I John 4:9-11 (NKJV)

The propitiator has paid the price for my redemption. As a result, redemption should accomplish at least two basic results. First, it means one has been set free from sin, along with the guilt and burden of it. Second, in being set free, one is released and set free to serve the Lord. Redemption necessitates commitment to Jesus Christ and the lifestyle he expects one to live. The role of the Church is to complement the work of redemption in and through the life of the believer. The Biblical Church and Christian has a mission. There must be a readiness and willingness to serve, not just the Lord Jesus Christ, but also to serve others as Jesus Christ had done.

One of the factors that can hinder the desire of the Biblical Church and Christian is a type of spiritual myopia. For those who have been afflicted with myopia, it means they have become short-sighted, or are lacking in foresight or intellectual insight. This can apply to the cultural erosion and deterioration that is occurring within our nation as a whole and the church in particular. A problem with being myopic is that the horizon of one has become very abbreviated. It is more individualized than seeing life from a heavenly perspective. It functions in a broader context of which one is a part.

For the Church, it can be too easy to fall into the snare of the Church at Laodicea, Revelation 3:15-19. As Jesus walks in the midst of the Church, He observes:

> I know your deeds; you are neither cold nor hot. How I wish you were one or the other. So, because you are lukewarm—neither hot nor cold—I am about to spit you out of My mouth! You say, I am rich; I have grown wealthy and need nothing. But you do not realize that you are wretched, pitiful, poor, blind, and naked. I counsel you to buy from Me gold refined by fire so that you may become rich, white garments so that you may be clothed and your shameful nakedness not exposed, and salve to anoint your eyes so that you may see. Those I love, I rebuke and discipline. Therefore, be earnest and repent.

The condition Jesus observes then, as well as now, that stands out is: "…you do not realize that you are wretched, pitiful, poor, blind, and naked."

How does a group of people get themselves to a point where there is a neglect of reality and it is no longer part of their consciousness or awareness? Is it due to their personal self-contentment? Have they fallen into the trap of comparing themselves with other organizations and rationalizing they are not as bad as the other group? Have they taken the Word of God for granted? If they have the Word of God available, they have it, why are no longer governing themselves by it? Have they allowed themselves to become an organization that has neglected or forgotten its calling, purpose, vision and mission? Has it lost its desire to emulate the Lord Jesus Christ in their lives?

The Church has drifted far from its foundational principles. The desire of God's people must be comparable to the plea and prayer of David in Psalm 85:5-7 (NASB) for spiritual revival,

> Will You be angry with us forever? Will You prolong Your anger to all generations? Will You not revive us again, that Your people may rejoice in You? Show us Your lovingkindness, O Lord, and grant us Your salvation.

David had a sense of the spiritual dearth (a scarcity or lack of something) that can so easily creep into one's life and Church, resulting in coldness to the things of God.

In this nation during the early 1700s, this had become the spiritual drift in the British-American colonies. Bursting on the scene were two dynamic men, Jonathan Edwards and George Whitfield. They were key to a spiritual revival that swept throughout the colonies. Jonathan Edwards, the Yale minister who refused to convert to the Church of England, became concerned that New Englanders were becoming far too concerned with worldly matters. It seemed to him that people found the pursuit of wealth to be more important than John Calvin's religious principles. Edwards forcefully declared: God was an angry judge, and humans were sinners! It was reported that he spoke with such fury and conviction that people flocked to listen. It became known as The Great Awakening. Out of that time of forceful declaration of God's Word came his sermon: Sinners in the Hands of an Angry God. Many people were brought to tears and came repenting of their sins against a Holy God.

In addition to Jonathan Edwards (1703-1758), George Whitefield (1714-1770) was a minister from Great Britain who toured the American colonies. An actor by training and with good stage presence, he would forcefully declare the word of God, weep with sorrow, and tremble with passion as he delivered his sermons. Colonists flocked by the thousands to hear him speak. He converted slaves and a few Native Americans. It was reported that the religious skeptic Benjamin Franklin had come to hear him speak in Philadelphia and was also impacted by what he heard. What was so unique about their ministry and sermons?

In part, it was a dramatic shift and break from the Church of England and the formalism, rituals and traditions it represented. Additionally, there was an emphasis on the centrality of Prayer. A servant of the Lord who is committed to Church Revitalization has shared: Prayer is the most critical and essential element in the DNA of a local church.

Martin Luther said: Prayer is the daily business of the Christian.

John Calvin said: We see that nothing is set before us as an object of expectation from the Lord which we are not enjoined to ask of Him in prayer.

John Wesley said: There is nothing without prayer.

In noting these formidable servants of the Lord, what do you believe should be your focus, desire, and commitment to implement? How important is awakening and revitalization to you?

In a moment of uncertainty, confusion and fear, a Psalmist penned these words, Psalm 44:23-26 (NIV),

> Awake, Lord! Why do you sleep? Rouse yourself! Do not reject us forever. Why do you hide your face and forget our misery and oppression? We are brought down to the dust; our bodies cling to the ground. Rise up and help us; rescue us because of your unfailing love.

Do you ever identify with the words of this Psalmist? He wrote about misery and oppression. His characterization was that of being brought low and down to the ground. It indicates a mindset of loss and defeat. How would you deal with his plight and condition?

Put yourself in the Psalmist's situation. You believe you have done everything that is right and proper before the Lord, but yet you feel rejected, forgotten and left alone in the midst of your personal apprehensions. Do you think God is sleeping and ignoring you? Have you allowed yourself to think of God in human terms rather than in supernatural realities? One of the primary errors is in thinking that God would ever be asleep and ignorant of the individual's plight. The reminder is firmly stated in Psalm 121:4-8 (ESV),

> Behold, he who keeps Israel will neither slumber nor sleep. The Lord is your keeper; the Lord is your shade on your right hand. The sun shall not strike you by day, nor the moon by night. The Lord will keep you from all evil; he will keep your life. The Lord will keep your going out and your coming in from this time forth and forevermore.

What causes one to be living in Psalm 44 rather than in Psalm 121? What does one need to have as a perspective from the Lord?

Dr. Harry Reeder has summarized in Embers To A Flame the revitalization concerns:

> The Scripture presents a paradigm of moving from spiritual decline and functional malaise to Spirit-engendered vitality: the Church at Ephesus. God's instructions to that church serve as a curriculum outline for Church Revitalization: Remember therefore from where you have fallen, and repent and do the deeds you did at first (Revelation 2:5). That is the three-fold paradigm: Remember. Repent. Recover (return to) the first things. Church revitalization or renewal is nothing more than following God's prescription for church health. It is a process by which we work at reformation, lead for revitalization and pray for revival. Church Revitalization is the sovereign work of God's Spirit whereby He restores His people to spiritual and functional vitality that inevitably leads to statistical growth in conversions and scriptural discipleship for His own glory and our own good.

Where does Awakening need to begin? With God? He neither slumbers nor sleeps! With you? Ephesians 5:14 states who will benefit from and who are among those whom The Light must awaken! Could it be that a malaise has inflicted those who are called God's People? Are we more oriented to the status quo than we are to God's Revitalization?

In Revelation 2:1-7, when the Lord is described as walking among the Churches, what is the primary area He points out about the Church at Ephesus? The threefold paradigm mentioned above is given to Remember, Repent, and Recover (return to first things). The focus the Lord shares with the Church is Revelation 2:4, "But I have this against you: You have abandoned your first love." These words need to be internalized by all of God's people today, "You have abandoned your first love." Is it possible that God's people no longer crave the intimacy, passion and presence of the Lord Jesus Christ in one's personal life? The very thought of it should penetrate deep within one's soul – "I no longer love the Lord as I once did!" Even if this is marginally correct, it should drive one to his/her knees before the Lord and remain there until correction is sought and becomes the reality. Is this something you need to do – now?

One concern of the Revivalist Preachers in the early 1700s was the state of worldliness that had been embraced by the people. Materialism had become the primary focus rather than Biblical adherence. There are many ways to describe the Culture and Church in America in the twenty-first century. Materialism and Worldliness stand out among a longer list of departures from Spiritual Verity and Commitments. That which seems to have become distorted and misrepresented is how great the drift has become in terms of worldliness. It seems as though the key words in I John 2:15-17 have been blotted out of the memory of many people today, and that includes professing Christians. What did John write and what did it mean? John wrote:

> Do not love the world or anything in the world. If anyone loves the world, the love of the Father is not in him. For all that is in the world—the desires of the flesh, the desires of the eyes, and the pride of life—is not from the Father but from the world. The world is passing away along with its desires, but whoever does the will of God remains forever.

The direct statement that should arouse concern among the professing Christians is: "If anyone loves the world, the love of the Father is not in him." Does that remind you of what the Lord stated to the Church at Ephesus in Revelation 2:4, "You have abandoned your first love." Jesus was very clear in what He stated and meant in The Sermon on the Mount, Matthew 6:19-21,

> Do not store up for yourselves treasures on earth, where moth and rust destroy, and where thieves break in and steal. But store up for yourselves treasures in heaven, where moth and rust do not destroy, and where thieves do not break in and steal. For where your treasure is, there your heart will be also.

In other words, Jesus wants us to focus on the eternal and not the temporal. Where is your focus? What are your values? How would Jesus Christ assess them? If the secular world was able to give a credible assessment of the professing Christ and the Church one was attending, what would be the primary impression that would be shared? Suppose the secularist could project your life and that of the church you attend in three dimension, what kind of picture would one view? Would it cause anyone to be ashamed?

The primary concern for the Biblical child of God is to know the Lord Jesus Christ as intimately as possible and to consciously walk and live in His presence each day. A theme verse for one's lie is Psalm 140:13, "Surely the righteous shall give thanks to your name; the upright shall dwell in your presence." Dwelling in the presence of God should be one's goal and reality. This is part of what it means to be unchained and free indeed.

A Worthy Goal and Prayer

My Desire To Be Like Jesus,
My Desire to be like Him.
His Spirit fill me, His love overwhelms me,
In deed and word, to be like Him.

Is this your desire? Do you want to be like Jesus in all areas of your life? Do you want your deeds and words to be His deeds and words in you and flowing out from you? As one who has been unchained and set free indeed, it can and should be the reality of your life. May you desire it and may God grant it!

21. My Spiritual Journey

> I count everything as loss because of the surpassing worth of knowing Christ Jesus my Lord. For his sake I have suffered the loss of all things and count them as rubbish, in order that I may gain Christ and be found in him, not having a righteousness of my own that comes from the law, but that which comes through faith in Christ, the righteousness from God that depends on faith, that I may know him and the power of his resurrection, and may share his sufferings, becoming like him in his death, that by any means possible I may attain the resurrection from the dead.
>
> Philippians 3:8-11

What does it mean to know Jesus Christ and to make known? What must take place for the image of God to be present in a person? What is entailed in spiritual awakening? Who must be desperate for a spiritual awakening? Must awakening begin in and among Church Leadership first? How can one's heart cry for revival be determined as being real or fictional?

Spiritual Awakening and Church Revitalization do not just happen without careful thought, preparation, effort and prayer. It requires godly people hungering for the presence of God and an outpouring of His Spirit in the lives of God's people. It is a desire for new life and vitality. It entails a vision of God's desires and an obedience to His directives. There needs to be a core of faithful men/witnesses (Second Timothy 2:2): "The things that you have heard me say among many witnesses, entrust these to faithful men who will be qualified to teach others as well."

Could it be that we are living in a day when the culture has so infiltrated the Church that godliness is no longer the norm nor the desire of men's hearts? Can this occur in the twenty-first century Church? Has it already taken place? Is it occurring and steadily increasing among professing Christians? Is the commentary about the Church the words of Micah 7:2, "the godly person has perished from the land, and there is no upright person among men."?

A practical contributor about the need for Spiritual Awakening and that which may hinder it is James Emory White. He began a Church Plant 25 years ago and has been Senior Pastor of the work from the beginning. In reflecting on those 25 years, he has written a soon to be published book – What They Didn't Teach You In Seminary. A portion of that book is in a current Blog form: "25 Years Of Leadership Lessons." Just a few of his "Lessons" are:

(1) Fads and styles, models and trendsetters, will come and go. Stay focused on one thing: the mission. (2) You'll grow bigger and faster if you focus on transfer growth. Don't. Reaching the unchurched is what it's all about.

> (3) On any and every issue, go to the Bible and then go with the Bible.
>
> (4) Prize character over talent, and loyalty over just about anything.
>
> (5) Resolve to prioritize children's ministry. Once again, you'll find it to be the Best. Decision. Ever.
>
> (6) The key question to ask isn't how to grow the church; the key question to ask is what is keeping the church from growing.
>
> (7) You don't possess every spiritual gift. Don't operate as if you do or let others expect it of you.
>
> (8) Your competition isn't, and never will be, another church. You're after the person who doesn't give a rip about churches.
>
> (9) Your core values are the hills you should die on.

> (10) Left to itself, the natural flow of the church is to turn inward, grow older and become outdated. Leadership must intentionally combat all three.

Too many churches that are dwindling continue to look inward and become maintenance type efforts. Caring for the "older" members is great but ministry must never be limited to doing just that. There is also a need to consider and evaluate the "leaders" of the particular congregation. Are they godly men of vision and prayer? The goal for leadership is summarized in Acts 6:4,

> Brothers and sisters, choose seven men from among you who are known to be full of the Spirit and wisdom. We will turn this responsibility over to them."

Was this a good decision? Would there be a good result from this action? Could ordinary men be enabled to accomplish the extraordinary in the name of Christ? An answer given is in Acts 6:6-7 (ESV),

> The apostles prayed and laid their hands on them. And the word of God continued to increase, and the number of the disciples multiplied greatly in Jerusalem, and a great many of the priests became obedient to the faith.

In 2005, Dr. Stephen Olford published a book: "Heart Cry for Revival: What Revivals Teach Us for Today." He wrote:

> Never was a church-wide, heaven-sent revival needed than at this present time. It is the only answer to the spiritual warfare we face in every part of the world. Bombs, bullets and body bags will never stem the tide of terror and horror that threatens human existence. We must recognize that: the weapons of our warfare are not carnal but mighty in God for pulling down strongholds, casting down arguments and every high thing that exalts itself against the knowledge of God,

bringing every thought into captivity to the obedience of Christ (Second Corinthians 10:4-5).

There is also a need to consider and evaluate the leaders of the particular congregation. Are they godly men of vision and prayer? A goal for leadership is summarized in Acts 6:4, "Brothers and sisters, choose seven men from among you who are known to be full of the Spirit and wisdom. We will turn this responsibility over to them." Was this a good decision? Would there be a good result from this action? There are a series of summary verses in the Book of Acts that characterize the result of a praying church and leadership. Can ordinary men accomplish the extraordinary in the name of Christ?

A first summary answer given is in Acts 6:6-7 (ESV), "The apostles prayed and laid their hands on them. And the word of God continued to increase, and the number of the disciples multiplied greatly in Jerusalem, and a great many of the priests became obedient to the faith."

A second summary verse is Acts 9:31 (BSB), "Then the church throughout Judea, Galilee, and Samaria experienced a time of peace. It grew in strength and numbers, living in the fear of the Lord and the encouragement of the Holy Spirit."

A third summary is Acts 12:23-24, "Herod, who opposed the Gospel and Paul refused to give glory to God, an angel of the Lord struck him down…But the word of God continued to spread and multiply. In the midst of challenge and adversity, God honored His Word, the Holy Spirit moved among the people, and rather that eradication there was multiplication.

A fourth summary is Acts 16:4-5, "As they went from town to town, they delivered the decisions handed down by the apostles and elders in Jerusalem for the people to obey. So, the churches were strengthened in the faith and grew daily in numbers." The key words in this summary are "strengthened" and "grew daily in numbers."

What do you think? Can this happen in your local Church, Community, Area? Has it ever been considered? Is there a readiness to make changes? When was the last time this criterion was the standard for spiritual leadership in your Church? Recently? Ever?

As and when a group gets back on track with the Lord's call, purpose, vision and mission, Revelation 3:20-21 indicates a renewed relationship with Jesus Christ: "Behold, I stand at the door and knock. If anyone hears My voice and opens the door, I will come in and dine with him, and he with Me. To the one who is victorious, I will grant the right to sit with Me on My throne, just as I overcame and sat down with My Father on His throne." What awaits one who responds to the words of Jesus? It involves relationship, fellowship, fruitfulness and victory.

Faith Is The Victory (John H. Yates – 1891) is a hymn that contains these words of reminder:

On every hand the foe we find;
Drawn up in dread array.
Let tents of ease be left behind,
And onward to the fray.

To him that overcomes the foe,
White raiment shall be given.
Before the angels he shall know
His name confessed in Heaven.
Then onward from the hill of light,
Our hearts with love aflame,
We'll vanquish all the hosts of night,
In Jesus' conquering Name.

This is your calling and opportunity. How will you respond to it? Will you maintain the status quo or cross over into Christ's victory for you, His people and His Church? Will you live in the reality of being unchained and free indeed? The words of a Sunday School Chorus should remain as one's ongoing commitment to Jesus Christ and the task He wants us to do.

After all He's done for me;
After all He's done for me;
How can I do less than give Him my best,
And live for Him completely,
After all He's done for me?

22. My Uniqueness

Now when they saw the boldness of Peter and John, and perceived that they were uneducated and untrained men, they marveled. And they realized that they had been with Jesus.

Acts 4:13 (NKJV)

Do you ever feel as though you are insignificant? Do you feel that you are ignored when you wished you had been noticed as one who has value, significance and can make a viable contribution within the culture if only you were given an opportunity? When we consider these same factors and feelings within a religious context, there is the same conclusion and reality present. Scripture forbids favoritism in any form or context. The principle for governing God's people is enunciated in Deuteronomy 1:17, "You shall not show partiality in judgment; you shall hear the small and the great alike." In terms of organized religion, especially the Biblical Church, the principle is also clearly stated, James 2:1-5 (NLT), "My dear brothers and sisters, how can you claim to have faith in our glorious Lord Jesus Christ if you favor some people over others?" When this occurs, James asks, "Have you not shown partiality among yourselves, and become judges with evil thoughts?" The NKJV states this principle unequivocally, "Do not hold the faith of our Lord Jesus Christ, the Lord of glory, with partiality."

A recent devotional by Charles R. Swindoll (May 6, 2018), *Important To God*, mentions these same factors and feelings:

> *Most folks struggle with feelings of insignificance from time to time. Larger-than-life athletes, greatly gifted film and television stars, brilliant students,*

accomplished singers, skillful writers, even capable ministers can leave us feeling intimidated, overlooked, and underqualified. For some, feeling insignificant is not simply a periodic battle; it is a daily grind! We know deep down inside we're valuable; but when we compare ourselves, we often come out on the short end...(It) forces us to ask the age-old questions: Who am I? Why am I here? Where do I fit? What does it matter?

In 1974, Francis Schaeffer wrote encouraging words for those who feel ignored or who are treated as being insignificant. In his book, No Little People, he wrote:

The Scriptures mention that much can come from little if the little is consecrated to God. There are no little people and no big people in the true spiritual sense, but only consecrated and unconsecrated people.

He went on to write that the question one should ask is: "Am I a genuine and fully committed person of God?" Rather than withdrawing from spiritual warfare and slipping into spiritual doldrums, this is the question people in all generations should prayerfully consider before the Lord.

I have always been encouraged by the words in Psalm 139:13-16 (NKJV), A Psalm of David, we read his sense of his personal significance and worth in the sight and presence of God:

You formed my inward parts; You covered me in my mother's womb. I will praise You, for I am fearfully and wonderfully made; Marvelous are Your works, And that my soul knows very well. My frame was not hidden from You, When I was made in secret, And skillfully wrought in the lowest parts of the earth. Your eyes saw my substance, being yet unformed. And in Your book, they all were written.

the days fashioned for me, when as yet there were none of them.

If one embraces the negative attitude of or treatment by others, viewing one as insignificant or inconsequential, it will allow for bitterness within one's mind, soul and spirit. It is always of benefit to remember that God created us in His image and wants the image to be seen in us who are Biblical Christians (Romans 8:29, Second Corinthians 3:18, Ephesians 4:24, Colossians 3:10). The Catechism for Young Children begins with questions about God and a person's uniqueness and significance: "Who made you? God! What else did God make? All things! Why did God make you and all things? For His own glory! How can you glorify God? By loving Him and doing what He commands! Why ought you to glorify God? Because he made me and takes care of me!"

One's uniqueness is never determined by external factors but by God's determinative will for one's life. The words spoken to and through Isaiah (49:3-4) should serve as an encouragement for God's people in all generations:

> *The Lord said to me: You are my servant...in whom I will be glorified. But I said: I have labored in vain; I have spent my strength for nothing and vanity; yet surely my right is with the Lord, and my recompense with my God.*

The New Living Translation paraphrase applies these verses more plainly and succinctly:

> *The Lord said to me, You are my servant and you will bring me glory. I replied: But my work seems so useless! I have spent my strength for nothing and to no purpose. Yet I leave it all in the Lord's hand; I will trust God for my reward.*

If only, we would convincingly say: "I leave it all in the Lord's hand; I will trust God for my reward." It should be remembered that the committed Biblical Christian is not serving man but God. One may go through his/her life and career with little or no notice by one's peers. It might include being passed over for a promotion, It could also mean not receiving special mention for an achievement or work done satisfactorily. It can hurt one deeply when others seem to get recognition when they are no more deserving, or maybe not as deserving, and you are overlooked or taken for granted. All should remember particular teaching of the Lord Jesus Christ in this regard. The Sermon on the Mount teaches, Matthew 7:21-23,

> *Not everyone who calls out to me, 'Lord! Lord!' will enter the Kingdom of Heaven. Only those who actually do the will of my Father in heaven will enter. On judgment day many will say to me, Lord! Lord! We prophesied in your name and cast out demons in your name and performed many miracles in your name. But I will reply: I never knew you. Get away from me, you who break God's laws.*

Similarly, The Olivet Discourse, Matthew 24 and 25, references the judgment scene at the coming again of the Lord Jesus Christ. Particularly, in Matthew 25:31-46, the separation of the sheep and goats. Jesus declares:

(Verses 31-33):

> *But when the Son of Man comes in his glory, and all the angels with him, then he will sit upon his glorious throne. All the nations will be gathered in his presence, and he will separate the people as a shepherd separates the sheep from the goats. He will place the sheep at his right hand and the goats at his left.*

This criterion of Jesus Christ is surprising to both the sheep and the goats. The righteous respond to it by asking (Verses 37-39):

> *Lord, when did we ever see you hungry and feed you? Or thirsty and give you something to drink? Or a stranger and show you hospitality? Or naked and give you clothing? When did we ever see you sick or in prison and visit you?*

These questions reflect on the earlier discussion raised in James 2 about favoritism. Jesus is observing in His discourse that the righteous did caring things in His name because of their commitment to Him. They did it as children of light. Their desire was to be certain that He would be glorified. They were committed to and engaged in the "least of these" ministry in His name.

Those designated as goats in Matthew 25:44-45 ask similar questions posed by the sheep but from a different perspective about needs and care. The goats replied:

> *Lord, when did we ever see you hungry or thirsty or a stranger or naked or sick or in prison, and not help you? And he will answer: I tell you the truth, when you refused to help the least of these my brothers and sisters, you were refusing to help me.*

In life, some are tempted to view such matters in terms of what difference does it make. The difference is in terms of eternity and what one believes about heaven and hell. If one is inclined to believe that all people (souls) will go to heaven, the teaching of Jesus Christ refutes that idea. As a matter of fact, Jesus clearly stated (Matthew 25:46), "And these (the goats) will go away into eternal punishment, but the righteous (the sheep) into eternal life."

What difference does it make? What is in the eternal balance of things that matter most and those things that do not matter? A worship chorus written by Alfred B. Smith (1941) that lends itself to one's motive and purpose contains these determinative words: "May I do each day's work for Jesus, With Eternity's values in view."

A dear servant of the Lord, Dr. Synesio Lyra, Jr., posts both words of hope and encouragement, as well as Prayers, on Facebook. A Prayer for The Lord's Day, May 6, 2018 was:

> *Grant, our God, that Your houses of worship will be packed with people eager to hear Your Truth, sing Your praises, and experience the communion of the saints before the watching world. May each have open ears and pliable hearts that shall appropriate Your message to affect every life. May we all express our contrition for evil deeds committed or duties left unfulfilled. May Your faithful experience newness of life as they take new, bold steps in Your direction with the aid of Your Holy Spirit! In Jesus' precious Name we pray! Amen.*

If the subject matter of this prayer was incorporated into the lives of professing Christians and the contemporary Church, it would be transformative. The problem pertains to the ever-increasing compromise with the cultural mores of the day. Biblical values and foundational principles are regularly set aside and ignored. Accommodation has become the silent mantra of many institutions where numeric and financial growth are seen as vital for existence.

Those who are loyal to Jesus Christ and grateful that He has unchained them and set them free indeed are viewed as oddities and subsequentially ignored. In life, one may be faced with rejection, cruelty, persecution, imprisonment or death. There may be times when those who should be applying Biblical principles and values do not. It may mean one being passed by and viewed as being insignificant. The bottom line for the child of God is hearing the significant words of The

Master: (Matthew 25:21, 23), "Well done, good and faithful servant! You have been faithful with a few things; I will put you in charge of many things. Enter into the joy of your master!"

O victory in Jesus, My Savior, forever.
He sought me and bought me
With His redeeming blood;
He loved me ere I knew Him
And all my love is due Him,
He plunged me to victory,
Beneath the cleansing flood.

Epilogue

Amid the several addictions present in our culture and world, some that have infiltrated the population world-wide are drugs and mood modifiers; pornography; abuse (both spousal and child); human trafficking; bullying; anger;

etc. From a psychological and spiritual potential, there are several more subtle, as well as blatant, addictions.

Psychologically, there are those given to an inferiority complex – the lack of self-worth; given to doubt and uncertainty about oneself; the belief that one does not measure up to suggested and imposed standards; antisocial behavior. There is a tendency to be given to self-pity and reluctance to ever try to demonstrate one's abilities and ideas lest such an effort will be rejected and the person subjected to a sense of being ridiculed as well as rejected.

Spiritually, there are several factors that impact one, regardless of Biblical teaching to the contrary. A previous chapter shared some thoughts on favoritism from the Book of James. James has clearly defined what favoritism is and why it is not implemented by Biblical standards and values. A careful reading of James 2 and 3 indicates areas for review, repentance and remedy. It is not uncommon to hear some older adult members of a church suggest about someone seeking to become part of the group – "They (or he/she/they) are not our kind of people." It's not always in the spoken word but in the body language of a person or group.

These types of behaviors can be experienced among the professional types. There is a tendency to allow a pecking order to be present within the Church in general and denominations in particular. There are the elite and erudite few who are allowed privileges denied to those deemed to be not as significant, capable or worthy. Perhaps you can be encouraged by the words of Charles R. Swindoll in Insight for Living, *God Controls The Details*: “How well does God know you? Completely! You need never again feel unimportant or insignificant.” The context of his thought is Psalm 139 and his discussion on the significance of God in the detail of one’s life, and the significance of a person whose confidence is in God alone.

While remaining at home on The Lord’s Day, I listened to a religious program from a dozen years ago. The opening anthem sung was current then but new to me. The words were written by Donnie McLurkin:

Holiness, holiness is what I long for;
Holiness is what I need.
Holiness, holiness is what You want from me.

Righteousness, righteousness is what You want for me,
So, Take my heart and mold it;
Take my mind, transform it;
Take my will, conform it; To Yours,
to Yours, Oh Lord.

Brokenness, brokenness is what I long for
Brokenness is what I need
Brokenness, brokenness is what You want
From me - For me.
So, take my heart and mold it
Take my mind and transform it
Take my will and conform it To Yours,
to Yours, oh, Lord.

Holiness, holiness is what I long for;
Holiness is what I know I need.
Holiness, holiness is what
You want from me.

In my devotional time, I like to refer to Hymns that come to mind. Among those that I find on-point were written by Horatius Bonar (1808-1889). He was a Scottish Presbyterian minister whose poems, hymns, and religious tracts were widely popular during the 19th century. One of the Hymns that apply to the theme of this book, Unchained Expectations, is titled *Not What My Hands Have Done* (1864).

Not what my hands have done,
Can save my guilty soul;
Not what my toiling flesh has borne
Can make my spirit whole.
Not what I feel or do, Can give me peace with God;
Not all my prayers, And sighs and tears
Can bear my awful load.

Thy work alone, O Christ, Can ease this weight of sin;
Thy blood alone O Lamb of God,
Can give me peace within.
Thy love to me O God, Not mine, O Lord, to Thee
Can rid me of This dark unrest,
And set my spirit free!

Thy grace alone, O God, To me can pardon speak;
Thy power alone O Son of God,
Can this sore bondage break.
No other work, save Thine, No other blood will do,
No strength save that, Which is divine,
Can bear me safely through.

I bless the Christ of God; I rest on love divine;
And with unfaltering lip and heart,
I call this Savior mine.
His cross dispels each doubt, I bury in His tomb
My unbelief, And all my fear,
Each lingering shade of gloom.

I praise the God of grace, I trust His truth and might;
He calls me His, I call Him mine,
My God, my joy, my light, 'Tis He Who saveth me,
And freely pardon gives.
I love because He loveth me,
I live because He lives!

This is the only pathway available for one to realize unchained expectations and to enjoy all of the benefits of being free indeed. Have you come to Jesus and sought Him and asked Him to shatter your chains, break your shackles and set you free indeed? In the words written by John M. Wigner (1871):

Come to the Savior now, He gently calls to you;
in true repentance bow, let him your heart renew.
Christ came that you may know
salvation, peace, and love,
true joy on earth below, a home in heaven above.

Come to the Savior, all, whate'er your burdens be;
hear now His loving call, "Cast all your care on me."
Come, and for every grief, in Jesus you will find
a sure and safe relief, a loving friend and kind.

About the Author

James Perry has served the Church with more than 54 years of continuous ministry. He attended Columbia Bible College (now Columbia International University) for three years; transferring to Covenant College, a new Presbyterian College in St. Louis, MO from which he graduated with a B.A. in Philosophy. After graduation, he enrolled in Covenant Theological Seminary where he received a B.D. in theology, and returned later for his M.A. He and his wife make their home in Centreville, AL; He has four children; 16 Grandchildren and 14 Great Grandchildren. He is the Author of 10 Books (all of which are available on Amazon).

About the Author

www.ingramcontent.com/pod-product-compliance
Lightning Source LLC
LaVergne TN
LVHW051503080426
835509LV00017B/1891

* 9 7 8 1 7 3 2 4 3 7 9 2 0 *